Consider Every Word

of

Jesus Christ

Volume 2

*

With God
All things are possible!

This is the second in   The Book Series to Consider

All scripture taken from King James Companion Bible 1611 with the Structures and Critical, Explanatory and Suggestive Notes and with 198 Appendixes

Though not endorsed by Shepherd's Chapel references made are with permission.

Printed in the United States of America

ISBN 978-0-9777851-3-1   volume 2

ISBN 978-0-9777851-7-9   volume 1&2

ISBN 978-0-9777851-6-2   four biblical book set

Coming soon   www.publishinggodsway.com

To contact us   publishinggodsway@bv.net   or
                     352-391-1959

THERE IS NO GREATER GIFT THAN THE
TRUE WORDS OF JESUS CHRIST

My gift to you

Occasion

From

Date

Dedication

This work is dedicated to all of God's children!

We have been told to search the scriptures. Not to just read, but to *search,* so that you too will understand the present times, as well as what is to come in our near future!

We have been given power over *all* of our enemies by God! Now, guess what? God wants us to know that we have many!

We have a job to do and not a lot of time to get it done! We cannot afford to be unaware any longer of the duty we have been given to serve Our Father by sharing His Word with others!

There is no need to be confused by the Tsunami or Katrina, the earthquakes, tornadoes or hurricanes. Yes, these events have occurred over the years but not as often or as close as they are occurring now!

We have been foretold all things (Mark 13:23) so there is no need to be afraid of, nor to be confused by anything!

Our Lord said you can discern the sky but you cannot tell the times? (Matthew 16:3)

It is time to wake up friends! It is time for biblical illiteracy to become a thing of the past by learning what Jesus had to say to us and then by sharing His Words with all that you know! Why?

So that they too may understand! This is why we are here!

Let's start reminding people everywhere to repent!

Author's Note

While Jesus Christ spoke the word multitude only twice, the word has been used about two hundred forty times in God's Word.

The gripping significance is that we have been here before in the first earth age!

We now live in the second earth age and those who endure to the end shall be saved (Matthew 10:22) and will continue into the eternity which is the third earth age!

Now, how fascinating is that? We are going to see the end of this earth age!

Now; we don't have to be afraid because with repentance and our belief on Jesus Christ, God is not mad at us!

Consider Every Word of Jesus Christ

Mk 4:37	And there arose a great storm of wind and the waves beat into the ship so that it was now full.
Mk 4:38	Master, carest thou not that we perish?
Mk 4:39	Peace be still. And the wind ceased and there was a great calm.
Mk 4:40	Why are ye so fearful? How is it that ye have no faith?

Mk 5:2	And when he was come out of he ship, immediately there met him out of the tombs a man with an unclean spirit.
Mk 5:7	And cried with a loud voice and said, What have I to do with thee, Jesus, thou Son of the most high God? I adjure thee by God that thou torment me not.
Mk 5:8	Come out of the man, thou unclean spirit.

Mk 5:9	What is thy name? And he answered, saying, My name is Legion: for we are many.
Mk 5:11	Now there was there nigh unto the mountains a great herd of swine feeding.
Mk 5:12	And all the devils besought him saying, Send us into the swine that we may enter into them.

1

Mk 5:13	And forthwith Jesus gave them leave. And the unclean spirits went out and entered into the swine: and the herd ran violently down a steep place into the sea, (they were about two thousand;) and were choked in the sea.
Mk 5:14	And they that fed the swine fled and told it in the city, and in the country. And they went out to see what it was that was done.
Mk 5:19	Go home to thy friends and tell them how great things the Lord hath done for thee and hath had compassion on thee.
Mk 5:22	And behold there cometh one of the rulers of the synagogue, Jairus by name; and when he saw Him, he fell at His feet.
Mk 5:23	And besought him greatly, saying My little daughter lieth at the point of death: I pray thee, come and lay thy hands on her, that she may be healed; and she shall live.
Mk 5:25	And a certain woman which had an issue of blood twelve years.
Mk 5:27	When she had heard of Jesus came in the press behind and touched his garment.
Mk 5:30	Who touched My clothes?

Mk 5:33	But the woman fearing and trembling, knowing what was done in her, came and fell down before Him and told Him all the truth.
Mk 5:34	Daughter, thy faith hath made thee whole; go in peace and be whole of thy plague.
Mk 5:35	While he yet spake, there came from the ruler of the synagogue's house certain which said, Thy daughter is dead: why troublest thou the Master any further?
Mk 5:36	Be not afraid, only believe.
Mk 5:39	Why make ye this ado and weep? The damsel is not dead but sleepeth.
Mk 5:41	Talitha cumi; which is being interpreted, Damsel, I say unto thee arise.
Mk 5:42	And straightway the damsel arose and walked for she was of the age of twelve years. And they were astonished with a great astonishment.
Mk 5:43	And He charged them straitly that no man should know it; and commanded that something should be given her to eat.
Mk 6:4	A prophet is not without honour, but in his own country and among his own kin and in his own house.

Mk 6:10   In what place soever ye enter into an house, there abide till ye depart from that place.

Mk 6:11   And whosoever shall not receive you nor hear you, when ye depart thence, shake off the dust under your feet for a testimony against them. Verily I say unto you, it shall be more tolerable for Sodom and Gomorrha in the day of judgment, than for that city.

Mk 6:30   And the apostles gathered themselves together unto Jesus, and told Him all things, both what they had done, and what they had taught.

Mk 6:31   Come ye yourselves apart into a desert place and rest a while: for there were many coming and going and they had no leisure so much as to eat.

Mk 6:34   And Jesus, when he came out, saw much people and was moved with compassion toward them, because they were as sheep not having a shepherd: and he began to teach them many things.

Mk 6:37   Give ye them to eat.

Mk 6:38   How many loaves have ye? Go and see.

Mk 6:41   And when he had taken the five loaves and the two fishes, he looked up to heaven and blessed and brake the loaves and gave them to his

4

disciples to set before them; and the two fishes divided he among them all.

Mk 6:42   And they did all eat and were filled.

Mk 6:47   And when even was come, the ship was in the midst of the sea and he alone on the land.

Mk 6:49   But when they saw him walking upon the sea, they supposed it had been a spirit and cried out:

Mk 6:50   Be of good cheer: it is I: be not afraid.

Mk 7:6   Well hath Esaias prophesied of you hypocrites, as it is written. This People honoureth Me with their lips but their heart is far from Me.

Mk 7.7   Howbeit in vain do they worship Me, teaching for doctrines the commandments of men.

Mk 7:8   For laying aside the commandment of God, ye hold the tradition of men as the washing of pots and cups: and many other such like things ye do.

Mk 7:9   Full well ye reject the commandment of God, that ye may keep your own tradition.

Mk 7:10   For Moses said, Honour thy father and thy mother; and, Whoso curseth father or mother, let him die the death:

Mk 7:11   But ye say, If a man shall say to his father or mother, It is Corban, (that is to say, a gift), by

	whatsoever thou mightest be profited by me; he shall be free.
Mk 7:12	And ye suffer him no more to do ought for his father or his mother;
Mk 7:13	Making the word of God of none effect through your tradition, which ye have delivered: and many such like things do ye.
Mk 7:14	Hearken unto Me every one of you and understand:
Mk 7:15	There is nothing from without a man, that entering into him can defile him? But the things which come out of him, those are they that defile the man.
Mk 7:16	If any man have ears to hear, let him hear.
Mk 7:18	Are ye so without understanding also? Do ye not perceive that whatsoever thing from without entereth into the man, it cannot defile him.
Mk 7:19	Because it entereth not into his heart, but into the belly, and goeth out into the draught, purging all meats?
Mk 7:20	That which cometh out of the man, that defileth the man.

Mk 7:21	For from within, out of the heart of men, proceed evil thoughts, adulteries, fornications, murders,
Mk 7:22	Thefts, covetousness, wickedness, deceit, lasciviousness, an evil eye, blasphemy, pride, foolishness:
Mk 7:23	All these evil things come from within, and defile the man.
Mk 7:25	For a certain woman, whose young daughter had an unclean spirit, heard of him and came and fell at his feet:
Mk 7:26	The woman was a Greek a Syrophenician by nation; and she besought him that he would cast forth the devil out of her daughter.
Mk 7:27	Let the children first be filled: for it is not meet to take the children's bread and to cast it unto the dogs.
Mk 7:28	And she answered and said unto him, Yes, Lord: yet the dogs under the table eat of the children's crumbs.
Mk 7:29	For this saying go thy way; the devil is gone out of thy daughter.
Mk 7:34	And looking up to heaven, he sighed, and saith unto him, Ephphatha, that is, Be opened.

Mk 8:2	I have compassion on the multitude because they have now been with Me three days, and have nothing to eat:
Mk 8:3	And if I send them away fasting to their own houses, they will faint by the way: for divers of them came from far.
Mk 8:5	How many loaves have ye?
Mk 8:6	And He commanded the people to sit down on the ground; and He took the seven loaves, and gave thanks, and brake, and gave to His disciples to set before them; and they did set them before the people.
Mk 8:11	And the Pharisees came forth, and began to question with Him, seeking of Him a sign from heaven, tempting Him.
Mk 8:12	Why doth this generation seek after a sign? Verily I say unto you, There shall no sign be given unto this generation.
Mk 8:15	Take heed, beware of the leaven of the Pharisees, and of the leaven of Herod.
Mk 8:17	Why reason ye, because ye have no bread? Perceive ye not yet, neither understand? Have ye your heart yet hardened?
Mk 8:18	Having eyes, see ye not? And having ears, hear ye not? And do ye not remember?

Mk 8:19	When I brake the five loaves among five thousand, how many baskets full of fragments took ye up?
Mk 8:20	And when the seven among four thousand, how many baskets full of fragments took ye up?
Mk 8:21	How is it that ye do not understand?
Mk 8:22	And He cometh to Bethsaida; and they bring a blind man unto Him, and besought Him to touch him.
Mk 8:25	After that He put His hands again upon his eyes, and made him look up: and he was restored, and saw every man clearly.
Mk 8:26	Neither go into the town, nor tell it to any in the town.
Mk 8:27	Whom do men say that I am?
Mk 8:29	But whom say ye that I am?
Mk 8:33	Get thee behind Me, Satan: for thou savourest not the things that be of God, but the things that be of men.
Mk 8:34	Whosoever will come after Me, let him deny himself and take up his cross and follow Me.
Mk 8:35	For whosoever will save his life shall lose it; but whosoever shall lose his life for My sake and the gospel's, the same shall save it.

Mk 8:36	For what shall it profit a man, if he shall gain the whole world, and lose his own soul?
Mk 8:37	Or what shall a man give in exchange for his soul?
Mk 8:38	Whosoever therefore shall be ashamed of Me and of My words in this adulterous and sinful generation of him also shall the Son of man be ashamed, when He cometh in the glory of His Father with the holy angels.
Mk 9:1	Verily I say unto you, That there be some of them that stand here, which shall not taste of death, till they have seen the kingdom of God come with power.
Mk 9:7	And there was a cloud that overshadowed them: and a voice came out of the cloud, saying, This is My beloved Son: hear Him.
Mk 9:11	Why say the scribes that Elias must first come?
Mk 9:12	Elias verily cometh first and restoreth all things; and how it is written of the Son of man that He must suffer many things and be set at nought.
Mk 9:13	But I say unto you, That Elias is indeed come and they have done unto him whatsoever they listed, as it is written of him.

Mk 9:16	What question ye with them?
Mk 9:17	And one of the multitude answered and said, Master, I have brought unto thee my son, which hath a dumb spirit;
Mk 9:19	O faithless generation, how long shall I be with you? How long shall I suffer you? Bring him unto Me.
Mk 9:21	How long is it ago since this came unto him? And he said, Of a child.
Mk 9:23	If thou canst believe, all things are possible to him that believeth.
Mk 9:24	And straightway the father of the child cried out and said with tears, Lord, I believe; help Thou mine unbelief.
Mk 9:25	Thou dumb and deaf spirit, I charge thee, come out of him and enter no more into him.
Mk 9:29	This kind can come forth by nothing but by prayer and fasting.
Mk 9:31	The son of man is delivered into the hands of men and they shall kill Him; and after that He is killed, He shall rise the third day.
Mk 9:33	What was it that ye disputed among yourselves by the way?
Mk 9:35	If any man desire to be first, the same shall be last of all and servant of all.

Mk 9:37	Whosoever shall receive one of such children in My name, receiveth Me: and whosoever shall receive Me, receiveth not Me, but Him That sent Me.
Mk 9:38	And John answered Him, saying, Master, we saw one casting out devils in thy name, and he followeth not us: and we forbad him, because he followeth not us.
Mk 9:39	Forbid him not; for there is no man which shall do a miracle in My name, that can lightly speak evil of me.
Mk 9:40	For he that is not against us is on our part.
Mk 9:41	For whosoever shall give you a cup of water to drink in My name, because ye belong to Christ, verily I say unto you, he shall not lose his reward.
Mk 9:42	And whosoever shall offend one of these little ones that believe in Me, it is better for him that a millstone were hanged about his neck and he were cast into the sea.
Mk 9:43	And if thy hand offend thee, cut it off: it is better for thee to enter into life maimed than having two hands to go into hell, into the fire that never shall be quenched:

Mk 9:44	Where their worm dieth not and the fire is not quenched.
Mk 9:45	And if thy foot offend thee, cut it off: it is better for thee to enter halt into life, than having two feet to be cast into hell, into the fire that never shall be quenched:
Mk 9:46	Where their worm dieth not and the fire is not quenched.
Mk 9:47	And if thine eye offend thee, pluck it out: it is better for thee to enter into the kingdom of God with one eye, than having two eyes to be cast into hell fire:
Mk 9.48	Where their worm dieth not and the fire is not quenched.
Mk 9:49	For every one shall be salted with fire, and every sacrifice shall be salted with salt.
Mk 9:50	Salt is good: but if the salt have lost his saltness, wherewith will ye season it? Have salt in yourselves and have peace one with another.
Mk 10:3	What did Moses command you?
Mk 10:5	For the hardness of your heart he wrote you this precept.

Mk 10:6	But from the beginning of the creation God made them male and female.
Mk 10:7	For this cause shall a man leave his father and mother and cleave to his wife;
Mk 10:8	And they twain shall be one flesh: so then they are no more twain, but one flesh,
Mk 10:9	What therefore God hath joined together, let not man put asunder.
Mk 10:11	Whosoever shall put away his wife and marry another, committeth adultery against her.
Mk 10:12	And if a woman shall put away her husband and be married to another, she committeth adultery.
Mk 10:13	And they brought young children to him that he should touch them: and his disciples rebuked those that brought them.
Mk 10:14	Suffer the little children to come unto Me and forbid them not: for of such is the kingdom of God.
Mk 10:15	Verily I say unto you, Whosoever shall not receive the kingdom of God as a little child, he shall not enter therein.
Mk 10:17	And when He was gone forth into the way, there came one running and kneeled to Him

	and asked Him, Good Master, what shall I do that I may inherit eternal life?
Mk 10:18	Why callest thou Me good? There is none good but one, that is God.
Mk 10:19	Thou knowest the commandments. Do not commit adultery, Do not kill, Do not steal, Do not bear false witness, Defraud not, Honour thy father and mother.
Mk 10:21	One thing that thou lackest: go thy way, sell whatsoever thou hast and give to the poor and thou shalt have treasure in heaven: and come take up the cross and follow Me.
Mk 10:23	How hardly shall they that have riches enter into the kingdom of God!
Mk 10:24	Children, how hard is it for them that trust in riches to enter into the kingdom of God!
Mk 10:25	It is easier for a camel to go through the eye of a needle than for a rich man to enter into the kingdom of God.
Mk 10:27	With men it is impossible but not with God: for with God all things are possible.
Mk 10:29	Verily I say unto you, There is no man that hath left house or brethren or sisters or father or mother or wife or children or lands for My sake and the gospel's.

Mk 10:30	But he shall receive an hundredfold now in this time, houses and brethren and sisters and mothers and children and lands with persecutions; and in the world to come eternal life.
Mk 10:31	But many that are first shall be last; and the last first.
Mk 10:33	Behold, we go up to Jerusalem: and the Son of man shall be delivered unto the chief priests and unto the scribes; and they shall condemn Him to death and shall deliver Him to the Gentiles:
Mk 10:34	And they shall mock Him and shall scourge Him and shall spit upon Him and shall kill Him: and the third day He shall rise again.
Mk 10:35	And James and John the sons of Zebedee, come unto him, saying Master, we would that thou shouldest do for us whatsoever we shall desire.
Mk 10:36	What would ye that I should do for you?
Mk 10:38	Ye know not what ye ask: can ye drink of the cup that I drink of? And be baptized with the baptism that I am baptized with?
Mk 10:39	Ye shall indeed drink of the cup that I drink of; and with the baptism that I am baptized withal shall ye be baptized:

Mk 10:40	But to sit on My right hand and on My left hand is not Mine to give; but it shall be given to them for whom it is prepared.
Mk 10:42	Ye know that they which are accounted to rule over the Gentiles exercise lordship over them; and their great ones exercise authority upon them.
Mk 10:43	But so shall it not be among you; but whosoever will be great among you, shall be your minister:
Mk 10:44	And whosoever of you will be the chiefest shall be servant of all.
Mk 10:45	For even the Son of man came not to be ministered unto, but to minister and to give His life a ransom for many.
Mk 10:46	And they came to Jericho: and as he went out of Jericho with his disciples and a great number of people, blind Bartimaeus, the son of Timaeus, sat by the highway side begging.
Mk 10:51	What wilt thou that I should do unto thee? The blind man said unto him, Lord, that I might receive my sight.
Mk 10:52	Go thy way; thy faith hath made thee whole.

Mk 11:2   Go your way into the village over against you: and as soon as ye be entered into it, ye shall find a colt tied, whereon never man sat; loose him and bring him.

Mk 11:3   And if any man say unto you, Why do ye this? Say ye that the Lord hath need of him; and straightway he will send him hither.

Mk 11:12   And on the morrow when they were come from Bethany, he was hungry:

Mk 11:14   No man eat fruit of thee hereafter forever.

Mk 11:15   And they come to Jerusalem: and Jesus went into the temple and began to cast out them that sold and bought in the temple and overthrew the tables of the moneychangers and the seats of them that sold doves;

Mk 11:17   Is it not written, My house shall be called of all nations the house of prayer? But ye have made it a den of thieves.

Mk 11:20   And in the morning as they passed by, they saw the fig tree dried up from the roots.

Mk 11:21   And Peter calling to rememberance saith unto Him, Master, behold, the fig tree which thou cursedst is withered away.

Mk 11:22   Have faith in God.

Mk 11:23   For verily I say unto you, That whosoever shall say unto this mountain, Be thou removed and be thou cast into the sea; and shall not doubt in his heart, but shall believe that those things which he saith shall come to pass: he shall have whatsoever he saith.

Mk 11:24   Therefore I say unto you, What things soever ye desire when ye pray, believe that ye receive them and ye shall have them.

Mk 11:25   And when ye stand praying, forgive, if ye have ought against any: that your Father also Which is in heaven may forgive you your trespasses.

Mk 11.26   But if ye do not forgive, neither will your Father Which is in heaven forgive your trespasses.

Mk 11:27   And they come again to Jerusalem: and as he was walking in the temple, there come to him the chief priests and the scribes and the elders,

Mk 11:28   And say unto him, By what auhority doest thou these things? And who gave thee this authority to do these things?

Mk 11:29   I will also ask of you one question and answer Me and I will tell you by what authority I do these things.

Mk 11:30	The baptism of John, was it from heaven or of men? Answer Me.
Mk 11:33	Neither do I tell you by what authority I do these things.

Mk 12:1	A certain man planted a vineyard and set an hedge about it and digged a place for the winefat and built a tower and let it out to husbandmen and went into a far country
Mk 12:2	And at the season he sent to the husbandmen a servant that he might receive from the husbandmen of the fruit of the vineyard.
Mk 12:3	And they caught him and beat him and sent him away empty.
Mk 12:4	And again he sent unto them another servant; and at him they cast stones and wounded him in the head and sent him away shamefully handled.
Mk 12:5	And again he sent another; and him they killed and many others; beating some and killing some.
Mk 12:6	Having yet therefore one son, his well-beloved, he sent him also last unto them, saying, They will reverence my son.

Mk 12:7   But those husbandmen said among themselves,
           This is the heir; come, let us kill him and the
           inheritance shall be ours.

Mk 12:8   And they took him and killed him and cast him
           out of the vineyard.

Mk 12:9   What shall therefore the lord of the vineyard
           do? He will come and destroy the husbandmen
           and will give the vineyard unto others.

Mk 12:10   And have ye not read this scripture: The stone
           which the builders rejected is become the head
           of the corner:

Mk 12:11   This was the Lord's doing, and it is marvellous
           in our eyes.

Mk 12:13   And they send unto him certain of the Pharisees
           and of the Herodians, to catch him in his words.

Mk 12:15   Why tempt ye Me? Bring Me a penny, that I
           may see it.

Mk 12:16   Whose is this image and superscription? And
           they said unto Him, Caesar's.

Mk 12:17   Render to Caesar the things that are Caesar's
           and to God the things that are God's.

Mk 12:18   Then come unto him the Saducees, which say
           there is no resurrection: and they asked him
           saying.

Mk 12:19	Master, Moses wrote unto us, If a man's brother die and leave his wife behind him and leave no children, that his brother should take his wife and raise up seed unto his brother.
Mk 12:24	Do ye not therefore err because ye know not the scriptures, neither the power of God?
Mk 12:25	For when they shall rise from the dead, they neither marry nor are given in marriage; but are as the angels which are in heaven.
Mk 12:26	And as touching the dead that they rise: have ye not read in the book of Moses how in the bush God spake unto him, saying, I am the God of Abraham and the God of Isaac and the God of Jacob?
Mk 12:27	He is not the God of the dead but the God of the living: ye therefore do greatly err.
Mk 12:29	The first of all the commandments is, Hear O Israel; The Lord our God is one Lord:
Mk 12:30	And thou shalt love the Lord thy God with all thy heart and with all thy soul and with all thy mind and with all thy strength: this is the first commandment.
Mk 12:31	And the second is like, namely this, Thou shalt love thy neighbour as thyself. There is none other commandment greater than these.

Mk 12:34	Thou art not far from the kingdom of God. And no man after that durst ask Him any question.
Mk 12:35	How say the scribes that Christ is the son of David?
Mk 12:36	For David himself said by the Holy Ghost, The Lord said to my Lord, sit Thou on My right hand till I make Thine enemies Thy footstool.
Mk 12:37	David therefore himself calleth him Lord; and whence is he then his son?
Mk 12:38	Beware of the scribes, which love to go in long clothing and love salutations in the marketplaces.
Mk 12:39	And the chief seats in the synagogues and the uppermost rooms at feasts:
Mk 12:40	Which devour widows houses and for a pretence make long prayers: these shall receive greater damnation.
Mk 12:42	And there came a certain poor widow, and she threw in two mites, which make a farthing.
Mk 12:43	Verily I say unto you, That this poor widow hath cast more in than all they which have cast into the treasury:

Mk 12:44   For all they did cast in of their abundance; but she of her want did cast in all that she had, even all her living.

Mk 13:2   Seest thou these great buildings? There shall not be left one stone upon another, that shall not be thrown down.

Mk 13:5   Take heed lest any man deceive you:

Mk 13:6   For many shall come in My name saying I am Christ; and shall deceive many.

Mk 13:7   And when ye shall hear of wars and rumours of wars, be ye not troubled: for such things must needs be; but the end shall not be yet.

Mk 13:8   For nation shall rise against nation and kingdom against kingdom: and there shall be earthquakes in divers places and there shall be famines and troubles: these are the beginnings of sorrows.

Mk 13:9   But take heed to yourselves: for they shall deliver you up to councils; and in the synagogues ye shall be beaten: and ye shall be brought before rulers and kings for My sake, for a testimony against them.

Mk 13:10   And the gospel must first be published among all nations.

Mk 13:11   But when they shall lead you and deliver you up, take no thought beforehand what ye shall speak, neither do ye premeditate: but whatsoever shall be given you in that hour, that speak ye: for it is not ye that speak, but the Holy Ghost.

Mk 13:12   Now the brother shall betray the brother to death and the father the son; and children shall rise up against their parents and shall cause them to be put to death.

Mk 13:13   And ye shall be hated of all men for My name's sake: but he that shall endure unto the end, the same shall be saved.

Mk 13:14   But when ye shall see the abomination of desolation, spoken of by Daniel the prophet, standing where it ought not (let him that readeth understand) then let them that be in Judaea flee to the mountains:

Mk 13:15   And let him that is on the housetop not go down into the house, neither enter therein, to take any thing out of his house:

Mk 13:16   And let him that is in the field not turn back again for to take up his garment.

Mk 13:17   But woe to them that are with child and to them that give suck in those days!

Mk 13:18	And pray ye that your flight be not in the winter.
Mk 13:19	For in those days shall be affliction such as was not from the beginning of the creation which God created unto this time, neither shall be.
Mk 13:20	And except that the Lord had shortened those days, no flesh should be saved: but for the elect's sake, whom He hath chosen, He hath shortened the days.
Mk 13:21	And then if any man shall say to you, Lo, here is Christ; or, lo He is there; believe him not:
Mk 13:22	For false Christs and false prophets shall rise and shall shew signs and wonders, to seduce, if it were possible, even the elect.
Mk 13:23	But take ye heed: behold, I have foretold you all things.
Mk 13:24	But in those days, after that tribulation, the sun shall be darkened and the moon shall not give her light,
Mk 13:25	And the stars of heaven shall fall and the powers that are in heaven shall be shaken.
Mk 13:26	And then shall they see the Son of man coming in the clouds with great power and glory.
Mk 13:27	And then shall He send His angels, and shall gather together His elect from the four winds,

	from the uttermost part of the earth to the uttermost part of heaven.
Mk 13:28	Now learn a parable of the fig tree; When her branch is yet tender and putteth forth leaves, ye know that summer is near:
Mk 13:29	So ye in like manner, when ye shall see these things come to pass, know that it is nigh, even at the doors.
Mk 13:30	Verily I say unto you that this generation shall not pass till all these things be done.
Mk 13:31	Heaven and earth shall pass away: but My words shall not pass away.
Mk 13:32	But of that day and that hour knoweth no man, no not the angels which are in heaven, neither the Son, but the Father.
Mk 13:33	Take ye heed, watch and pray: for ye know not when the time is.
Mk 13:34	For the Son of man is as a man taking a far journey, who left his house and gave authority to his servants and to every man his work and commanded the porter to watch.
Mk 13:35	Watch ye therefore: for ye know not when the master of the house cometh, at even, or at midnight, or at the cockcrowing or in the morning:

Mk 13:36   Lest coming suddenly he find you sleeping.
Mk 13:37   And what I say unto you I say unto all, Watch.

Mk 14:3   And being in Bethany in the house of Simon
the leper, as he sat at meat, there came a
woman having an alabaster box of ointment of
spikenard very precious: and she brake the box
and poured it on his head.
Mk 14:4   And there were some that had indignation
within themselves and said, Why was this
waste of the ointment made?
Mk 14:5   For it might have been sold for more than three
hundred pence and have been given to the poor.
And they murmured against her.
Mk 14:6   Let her alone; why trouble ye her? She hath
wrought a good work on Me.
Mk 14:7   For ye have the poor with you always, and
whensoever ye will ye may do them good: but
Me ye have not always.
Mk 14:8   She hath done what she could; she is come
aforehand to anoint My body to the burying.
Mk 14:9   Verily I say unto you Wheresoever this gospel
shall be preached throughout the whole world,
this also that she hath done shall be spoken of
for a memorial of her.

Mk 14:13	And he sendeth forth two of his disciples and saith unto them, Go ye into the city and there shall meet you a man bearing a pitcher of water: follow him.
Mk 14:14	And wheresoever he shall go in, say ye to the Goodman of the house, The Master saith, Where is the guestchamber where I shall eat the Passover with My disciples?
Mk 14:15	And he will shew you a large upper room furnished and prepared: there make ready for us.
Mk 14:18	Verily I say unto you, One of you which eateth with Me shall betray Me.
Mk 14:20	It is one of the twelve that dippeth with Me in the dish.
Mk 14:21	The Son of man indeed goeth, as it is written of Him: but woe to that man by whom the Son of man is betrayed! Good were it for that man if he had never been born.
Mk 14:22	Take, eat: this is My body.
Mk 14:24	This is My blood of the new testament, which is shed for many.
Mk 14:25	Verily I say unto you, I will drink no more of the fruit of the vine until that day, that I drink it new in the kingdom of God.

Mk 14:27	All ye shall be offended because of Me this night: for it is written, I will smite the shepherd and the sheep shall be scattered.
Mk 14:28	But after that I am risen, I will go before you into Galilee.
Mk 14:30	Verily I say unto thee, That this day even in this night, before the cock crow twice, thou shalt deny Me thrice.
Mk 14:32	Sit ye here, while I shall pray.
Mk 14:34	My soul is exceeding sorrowful unto death: tarry ye here, and watch.
Mk 14:36	Abba, Father, all things are possible unto Thee; take away this cup from me: nevertheless not what I will, but what Thou wilt.
Mk 14:37	Simon, sleepest thou? Couldest not thou watch one hour?
Mk 14:38	Watch ye and pray lest ye enter into temptation. The spirit truly is ready, but the flesh is weak.
Mk 14:41	Sleep on now and take your rest: it is enough, the hour is come; behold the Son of man is betrayed into the hands of sinners.
Mk 14:42	Rise up, let us go; lo he that betrayeth Me is at hand.
Mk 14:43	And immediately, while he yet spake, cometh Judas, one of the twelve and with him a great

	multitude with swords and staves from the chief priests and the scribes and the elders.
Mk 14:48	Are ye come out as against a thief, with swords and with staves to take Me?
Mk 14:49	I was daily with you in the temple teaching and ye took Me not: but the scriptures must be fulfilled.
Mk 14:62	I am: and ye shall see the Son of man sitting on the right hand of power and coming in the clouds of heaven.
Mk 15:2	Thou sayest it.
Mk 15:34	Eloi, Eloi, lama sabachthani? Which is being interpreted, My God, My God, why hast Thou forsaken Me?
Mk 16:09	Now when Jesus was risen early the first day of the week, he appeared first to Mary Magdalene, out of whom he had cast seven devils.
Mk 16:11	And they, when they had heard that He was alive and had been seen of her, believed not.
Mk 16:15	Go ye into all the world and preach the gospel to every creature.
Mk 16:16	He that believeth and is baptized shall be saved but he that believeth not shall be damned.

Mk 16:17   And these signs shall follow them that believe:
            In My name shall they cast out devils: they
            shall speak with new tongues:

Mk 16:18   They shall take up serpents; and if they drink
            any deadly thing, it shall not hurt them; they
            shall lay hands on the sick, and they shall
            recover.

Mk 16:19   So then after the Lord had spoken unto them,
            he was received up into heaven and sat on the
            right hand of God.

Mt 1:17   So all the generations from Abraham to David
            are fourteen generations; and from David until
            the carrying away into Babylon are fourteen
            generations; and from the carrying away into
            Babylon unto Christ are fourteen generations.

Mt 3:15   Suffer it to be so now: for thus it becometh us
            to fulfill all righteousness.

Mt 4:4   It is written, Man shall not live by bread alone,
            but by every word that proceedeth out of the
            mouth of God.

Mt 4:7   It is written again, Thou shalt not tempt the
            Lord thy God.

Mt 4:10	Get thee hence, Satan: for it is written, Thou shalt worship the Lord thy God and Him only shalt thou serve.
Mt 4:17	Repent: for the kingdom of heaven is at hand.
Mt 4:19	Follow Me and I will make you fishers of men.
Mt 5:3	Blessed are the poor in spirit: for theirs is the kingdom of heaven.
Mt 5:4	Blessed are they that mourn: for they shall be comforted.
Mt 5:5	Blessed are the meek: for they shall inherit the earth.
Mt 5:6	Blessed are they which do hunger, and thirst after righteousness: for they shall be filled.
Mt 5:7	Blessed are the merciful: for they shall obtain mercy.
Mt 5:8	Blessed are the pure in heart: for they shall see God.
Mt 5:9	Blessed are the peacemakers: for they shall be called the children of God.
Mt 5:10	Blessed are they which are persecuted for righteousness sake: for theirs is the kingdom of heaven.

Mt 5:11   Blessed are ye, when men shall revile you and
           persecute you and shall say all manner of evil
           against you falsely, for My sake.

Mt 5:12   Rejoice and be exceeding glad: for great is your
           reward in heaven: for so persecuted they the
           prophets which were before you.

Mt 5:13   Ye are the salt of the earth: but if the salt have
           lost his savour, wherewith shall it be salted? It
           is thenceforth good for nothing, but to be cast
           out and to be trodden under foot of men.

Mt 5:14   Ye are the light of the world. A city that is set
           on a hill cannot be hid.

Mt 5:15   Neither do men light a candle and put it under a
           bushel but on a candlestick; and it giveth light
           unto all that are in the house.

Mt 5:16   Let your light so shine before men, that they
           may see your good works and glorify your
           Father Which is in heaven.

Mt 5:17   Think not that I am come to destroy the law or
           the prophets: I am not come to destroy but to
           fulfill.

Mt 5:18   For verily I say unto you, Till heaven and earth
           pass, one jot or one tittle shall in no wise pass
           from the law, till all be fulfilled.

Mt 5:19	Whosoever therefore shall break one of these least commandments and shall teach men, he shall be called the least, in the kingdom of heaven: but whosoever shall do and teach them, the same shall be called great in the kingdom of heaven.
Mt 5:20	For I say unto you, That except your righteousness shall exceed the righteousness of the scribes and Pharisees, ye shall in no case enter into the kingdom of heaven.
Mt 5:21	Ye have heard that it was said by them of old time, Thou shalt not kill; and whosoever shall kill shall be in danger of the judgment:
Mt 5:22	But I say unto you, That whosoever is angry with his brother without a cause shall be in danger of the judgment: and whosoever shall say to his brother, Raca, shall be in danger of the council: but whosoever shall say, Thou fool, shall be in danger of hell fire.
Mt 5:23	Therefore if thou bring thy gift to the altar and there rememberest that thy brother hath ought against thee;
Mt 5:24	Leave there thy gift before the altar and go thy way; first be reconciled to thy brother and then come and offer thy gift.

Mt 5:25	Agree with thine adversary quickly, whiles thou art in the way with him lest at any time the adversary deliver thee to the judge and the judge deliver thee to the officer and thou be cast into prison.
Mt 5:26	Verily I say unto thee, Thou shalt by no means come out hence, till thou hast paid the uttermost farthing.
Mt 5:27	Ye have heard that it was said by them of old time, Thou shalt not commit adultery:
Mt 5:28	But I say unto you, That whosoever looketh on a woman to lust after her hath committed adultery with her already in his heart.
Mt 5:29	And if thy right eye offend thee, pluck it out and cast it from thee: for it is profitable for thee that one of thy members should perish and not that thy whole body should be cast into hell.
Mt 5:30	And if thy right hand offend thee, cut it off and cast it from thee; for it is profitable for thee that one of thy members should perish and not that thy whole body should be cast into hell.
Mt 5:31	It hath been said, Whosoever shall put away his wife, let him give her a writing of divorcement:
Mt 5:32	But I say unto you, That whosoever shall put away his wife, saving for the cause of

fornication, causeth her to commit adultery: and whosoever shall marry her that is divorced committeth adultery.

Mt 5:33   Again, ye have heard that it hath been said by them of old time, Thou shalt not forswear thyself, but shalt perform unto the Lord thine oaths:

Mt 5:34   But I say unto you, Swear not at all; neither by heaven for it is God's throne:

Mt 5:35   Nor by the earth; for it is His footstool: neither by Jerusalem; for it is the city of the great King.

Mt 5:36   Neither shalt thou swear by thy head, because thou canst not make one hair white or black.

Mt 5:37   But let your communication be, Yea, yea; Nay, nay, for whatsoever is more than these cometh of evil.

Mt 5:38   Ye have heard that it hath been said, An eye for an eye and a tooth for a tooth:

Mt 5:39   But I say unto you, That ye resist not evil: but whosoever shall smite thee on thy right check, turn to him the other also.

Mt 5:40   And if any man will sue thee at the law, and take away thy coat, let him have thy cloke also.

Mt 5:41   And whosoever shall compel thee to go a mile, go with him twain.

Mt 5:42	Give to him that asketh thee and from him that would borrow of thee turn not, thou away.
Mt 5:43	Ye have heard that it hath been said, Thou shalt love thy neighbour and hate thine enemy.
Mt 5:44	But I say unto you, Love your enemies, bless them that curse you, do good to them that hate you and pray for them which despitefully use you and persecute you;
Mt 5:45	That ye may be the children of your Father Which is in heaven: for He maketh His sun to rise on the evil and on the good and sendeth rain on the just and on the unjust.
Mt 5:46	For if ye love them which love you what reward have ye? Do not even the publicans the same?
Mt 5:47	And if ye salute your brethren only, what do ye more than others? Do not even the publicans so?
Mt 5:48	Be ye therefore perfect, even as your Father Which is in heaven is perfect.
Mt 6:1	Take heed that ye do not your alms before men to be seen of them: otherwise ye have no reward of your Father Which is in heaven.

Mt 6:2	Therefore when thou doest thine alms, do not sound a trumpet before thee as the hypocrites do in the synagogues and in the streets, that they may have glory of men. Verily I say unto you, They have their reward.
Mt 6:3	But when thou doest alms, let not thy left hand know what thy right hand doeth:
Mt 6:4	That thine alms may be in secret: and thy Father Which seeth in secret Himself shall reward thee openly.
Mt 6:5	And when thou prayest, thou shalt not be as the hypocrites are; for they love to pray standing in the synagogues and in the corners of the streets, that they may be seen of men. Verily I say unto you, They have their reward.
Mt 6:6	But thou, when thou prayest, enter into thy closet and when thou hast shut thy door pray to thy Father Which is in secret; and thy Father Which seeth in secret shall reward thee openly.
Mt 6:7	But when ye pray, use not vain repetitions as the heathen do; for they think that they shall be heard for their much speaking.
Mt 6:8	Be not ye therefore like unto them: for your Father knoweth what things ye have need of, before ye ask Him.

Mt 6:9	After this manner therefore pray ye: Our Father Which art in heaven, Hallowed be Thy name.
Mt 6:10	Thy kingdom come, Thy will be done in earth as it is in heaven.
Mt 6:11	Give us this day our daily bread.
Mt 6:12	And forgive us our debts as we forgive our debtors.
Mt 6:13	And lead us not into temptation but deliver us from evil: For Thine is the kingdom and the power and the glory for ever. Amen.
Mt 6:14	For if ye forgive men their trespasses, your heavenly Father will also forgive you:
Mt 6:15	But if ye forgive not men their trespasses, neither will your Father forgive your trespasses.
Mt 6:16	Moreover when ye fast, be not as the hypocrites of a sad countenance: for they disfigure their faces that they may appear unto men to fast. Verily I say unto you, They have their reward.
Mt 6:17	But thou, when thou fastest, anoint thine head and wash thy face;
Mt 6:18	That thou appear not unto men to fast but unto thy Father Which is in secret: and thy Father, Which seeth in secret, shall reward thee openly.

Mt 6:19	Lay not up for yourselves treasures upon earth, where moth and rust doth corrupt and where thieves break through and steal:
Mt 6:20	But lay up for yourselves treasures in heaven, where neither moth nor rust doth corrupt and where thieves do not break through nor steal:
Mt 6:21	For where your treasure is, there will your heart be also.
Mt 6:22	The light of the body is the eye: if therefore thine eye be single, thy whole body shall be full of light.
Mt 6:23	But if thine eye be evil, thy whole body shall be full of darkness. If therefore the light that is in thee be darkness, how great is that darkness!
Mt 6:24	No man can serve two masters: for either he will hate the one and love the other: or else he will hold to the one and despise the other. Ye cannot serve God and mammon.
Mt 6:25	Therefore I say unto you, Take no thought for your life what ye shall eat, or what ye shall drink; nor yet for your body, what ye shall put on. Is not the life more than meat and the body than raiment?
Mt 6:26	Behold the fowls of the air: for they sow not neither do they reap, nor gather into barns; yet

your heavenly Father feedeth them. Are ye not much better than they?

Mt 6:27   Which of you by taking thought can add one cubit unto his stature?

Mt 6:28   And why take ye thought for raiment? Consider the lilies of the field, how they grow; they toil not, neither do they spin:

Mt 6:29   And yet I say unto you, That even Solomon in all his glory was not arrayed like one of these.

Mt 6:30   Wherefore, if God so clothe the grass of the field, which today is and tomorrow is cast into the oven, shall He not much more clothe you, O ye of little faith?

Mt 6:31   Therefore take no thought, saying, What shall we eat? Or, What shall we drink? Or, Wherewithal shall we be clothed?

Mt 6:32   For after all these things do the Gentiles seek: for your heavenly Father knoweth that ye have need of all these things.

Mt 6:33   But seek ye first the kingdom of God and His righteousness; and all these things shall be added unto you.

Mt 6:34   Take therefore no thought for the morrow: for the morrow shall take thought for the things of itself. Sufficient unto the day is the evil thereof.

Mt 7:1	Judge not that ye be not judged.
Mt 7:2	For with what judgment ye judge, ye shall be judged: and with what measure ye mete, it shall be measured to you again.
Mt 7:3	And why beholdest thou the mote that is in thy brother's eye, but considerest not the beam that is in thine own eye?
Mt 7:4	Or how wilt thou say to thy brother, Let me pull out the mote out of thine eye: and behold a beam is in thine own eye?
Mt 7:5	Thou hypocrite, first cast out the beam out of thine own eye: and then shalt thou see clearly to cast out the mote out of thy brother's eye.
Mt 7:6	Give not that which is holy unto the dogs, neither cast ye your pearls before swine, lest they trample them under their feet, and turn again and rend you.
Mt 7:7	Ask and it shall be given you; seek and ye shall find; knock and it shall be opened unto you:
Mt 7:8	For every one that asketh receiveth; and he that seeketh findeth; and to him that knocketh it shall be opened.

Mt 7:9	Or what man is there of you, whom if his son ask bread, will he give him a stone?
Mt 7:10	Or if he ask a fish, will he give him a serpent?
Mt 7:11	If ye then, being evil, know how to give good gifts unto your children, how much more shall your Father Which is in heaven give good things to them that ask Him?
Mt 7:12	Therefore all things whatsoever ye would that men should do to you, do ye even so to them: for this is the law and the prophets.
Mt 7:13	Enter ye in at the strait gate: for wide is the gate and broad is the way, that leadeth to destruction and many there be which go in thereat:
Mt 7:14	Because strait is the gate and narrow is the way, which leadeth unto life and few there be that find it.
Mt 7:15	Beware of false prophets, which come to you in sheep's clothing, but inwardly they are ravening wolves.
Mt 7:16	Ye shall know them by their fruits. Do men gather grapes of thorns, or figs of thistles?
Mt 7:17	Even so every good tree bringeth forth good fruit: but a corrupt tree bringeth forth evil fruit.
Mt 7:18	A good tree can not bring forth evil fruit, neither can a corrupt tree bring forth good fruit.

Mt 7:19	Every tree that bringeth not forth good fruit is hewn down and cast into the fire.
Mt 7:20	Wherefore by their fruits ye shall know them.
Mt 7:21	Not every one that saith unto Me, Lord, Lord, shall enter into the kingdom of heaven; but he that doeth the will of My father Which is in heaven.
Mt 7:22	Many will say to Me in that day, Lord, Lord, have we not prophesied in Thy name? And in Thy name have cast out devils? And in Thy name done many wonderful works?
Mt 7:23	And then will I profess unto them, I never knew you: depart from Me, ye that work iniquity.
Mt 7:24	Therefore whosoever heareth these sayings of Mine and doeth them, I will liken him unto a wise man which built his house upon a rock:
Mt 7:25	And the rain descended and the floods came and the winds blew and beat upon that house; and it fell not: for it was founded upon a rock.
Mt 7:26	And every one that heareth these sayings of Mine and doeth them not shall be likened unto a foolish man which built his house upon the sand:

Mt 7:27 And the rain descended and the floods came
     and the winds blew and beat upon that house
     and it fell: and great was the fall of it.

Mt 8:2 And behold, there came a leper and worshipped
     him, saying, Lord, if thou wilt, thou canst make
     me clean.

Mt 8:3 And Jesus put forth his hand and touched him,
     saying, I will: be thou clean. And immediately
     his leprosy was cleansed.

Mt 8:4 See thou tell no man: but go thy way, shew
     thyself to the priest and offer the gift that
     Moses commanded for a testimony unto them.

Mt 8:5 And when Jesus was entered into Capernaum
     there came unto him a centurion, beseeching
     him.

Mt 8:6 And saying, Lord, my servant lieth at home
     sick of the palsy, grievously tormented.

Mt 8:7 I will come and heal him.

Mt 8:10 Verily I say unto you, I have not found so great
     faith, no not in Israel.

Mt 8:11 And I say unto you, That many shall come
     from the east and west and shall sit down with

	Abraham and Isaac and Jacob in the kingdom of heaven.
Mt 8:12	But the children of the kingdom shall be cast out into outer darkness; there shall be weeping and gnashing of teeth.
Mt 8:13	Go thy way; and as thou hast believed, so be it done unto thee.
Mt 8:20	The foxes have holes and the birds of the air have nests; but the Son of Man hath not where to lay His head.
Mt 8:22	Follow Me; and let the dead bury their dead.
Mt 8:23	And when He was entered into a ship His disciples followed Him.
Mt 8:24	And behold, there arose a great tempest in the sea, insomuch that the ship was covered with the waves: but he was asleep.
Mt 8:25	And his disciples came to him and awoke him, saying, Lord, save us: we perish.
Mt 8:26	Why are ye fearful. O ye of little faith? Then he arose and rebuked the winds and the sea; and there was a great calm.
Mt 8:27	But the men marveled, saying. What manner of man is this, that even the winds and the sea obey him!

Mt 9:2	And behold, they brought to him a man sick of the palsy, lying on a bed: and Jesus seeing their faith said unto the sick of the palsy: Son, be of good cheer; thy sins be forgiven thee.
Mt 9:3	And, behold, certain of the scribes said within themselves, This man blasphemeth.
Mt 9:4	And Jesus knowing their thoughts said, Wherefore think ye evil in your hearts?
Mt 9:5	For whether is easier, to say, Thy sins be forgiven thee; or to say, Arise and walk?
Mt 9:6	But that ye may know that the Son of man hath power on earth to forgive sins, Arise, take up thy bed and go unto thine house.
Mt 9:9	Follow Me.
Mt 9:12	They that be whole need not a physician, but they that are sick.
Mt 9:13	But go ye and learn what that meaneth, I will have mercy and not sacrifice: for I am not come to call the righteous, but sinners to repentance.
Mt 9:15	Can the children of the bridechamber mourn as long as the bridegroom is with them? But the days will come when the bridegroom shall be taken from them and then shall they fast.

Mt 9:16	No man putteth a piece of new cloth unto an old garment for that which is put in to fill it up taketh from the garment and the rent is made worse.
Mt 9:17	Neither do men put new wine into old bottles: else the bottles break and the wine runneth out and the bottles perish: but they put new wine into new bottles and both are preserved.
Mt 9:18	While He spake these things unto them, behold, there came a certain ruler, and worshipped him, saying, My daughter is even now dead: but come and lay thy hand upon her, and she shall live.
Mt 9:22	Daughter, be of good comfort; thy faith hath made thee whole.
Mt 9:24	Give place: for the maid is not dead but sleepeth.
Mt 9:28	Believe ye that I am able to do this?
Mt 9:29	According to your faith be it unto you.
Mt 9:30	See that no man know it.
Mt 9:36	But when He saw the multitudes, He was moved with compassion on them, because they fainted, and were scattered abroad, as sheep having no shepherd.

Mt 9:37	The harvest truly is plenteous, but the labourers are few;
Mt 9:38	Pray ye therefore the Lord of the harvest, that He will send forth labourers into His harvest.
Mt 10:5	Go not into the way of the Gentiles and into any city of the Samaritans enter ye not:
Mt 10:6	But go rather to the lost sheep of the house of Israel.
Mt 10:7	And as ye go, preach, saying, The kingdom of heaven is at hand.
Mt 10:8	Heal the sick, cleanse the lepers, raise the dead, cast out devils: freely ye have received, freely give.
Mt 10:9	Provide neither gold, nor silver, nor brass in your purses,
Mt 10:10	Nor scrip for your journey, neiter two coats, neither shoes, nor yet staves: for the workman is worthy of his meat.
Mt 10:11	And into whatsoever city or town ye shall enter, inquire who in it is worthy; and there abide till ye go thence.
Mt 10:12	And when ye come into an house, salute it.

Mt 10:13	And if the house be worthy, let your peace come upon it: but if it be not worthy, let your peace return to you.
Mt 10:14	And whosoever shall not receive you, nor hear your words, when ye depart out of that house or city, shake off the dust of your feet.
Mt 10:15	Verily I say unto you, It shall be more tolerable for the land of Sodom and Gomorrha in the day of judgment, than for that city.
Mt 10:16	Behold, I send you forth as sheep in the midst of wolves: be ye therefore wise as serpents and harmless as doves.
Mt 10:17	But beware of men: for they will deliver you up to the councils and they will scourge you in their synagogues;
Mt 10:18	And ye shall be brought before governors and kings for My sake, for a testimony against them and the Gentiles.
Mt 10:19	But when they deliver you up, take no thought how or what ye shall speak: for it shall be given you in that same hour what ye shall speak.
Mt 10:20	For it is not ye that speak, but the Spirit of your Father Which speaketh in you.
Mt 10:21	And the brother shall deliver up the brother to death and the father the child and the children

shall rise up against their parents and cause them to be put to death.

Mt 10:22 And ye shall be hated of all men for My name's sake: but he that endureth to the end shall be saved.

Mt 10:23 But when they persecute you in this city, flee ye into another: for verily I say unto you, Ye shall not have gone over the cities of Israel, till the Son of man be come.

Mt 10:24 The disciple is not above his master, nor the servant above his lord.

Mt 10:25 It is enough for the disciple that he be as his master and the servant as his lord. If they have called the master of the house Beelzebub, how much more shall they call them of his household?

Mt 10:26 Fear them not therefore: for there is nothing covered that shall not be revealed; and hid, that shall not be known.

Mt 10:27 What I tell you in darkness, that speak ye in light: and what ye hear in the ear, that preach ye upon the housetops.

Mt 10:28	And fear not them which kill the body, but are not able to kill the soul; but rather fear Him Which is able to destroy both soul and body in hell.
Mt 10:29	Are not two sparrows sold for a farthing? And one of them shall not fall on the ground without your Father.
Mt 10:30	But the very hairs of your head are all numbered.
Mt 10:31	Fear ye not therefore, ye are of more value than many sparrows.
Mt 10:32	Whosoever therefore shall confess Me before men him will I confess also before My Father Which is in heaven.
Mt 10:33	But whosoever shall deny Me before men, him will I also deny before My Father Which is in heaven.
Mt 10:34	Think not that I am come to send peace on earth: I came not to send peace, but a sword.
Mt 10:35	For I am come to set a man at variance against his father, and the daughter against her mother, and the daughter in law against her mother in law.
Mt 10:36	And a man's foes shall be they of his own household.

Mt 10:37	He that loveth father or mother more than Me is not worthy of Me: and he that loveth son or daughter more than Me is not worthy of Me.
Mt 10:38	And he that taketh not his cross and followeth after Me, is not worthy of Me.
Mt 10:39	He that findeth his life shall lose it: and he that loseth his life for My sake shall find it.
Mt 10:40	He that receiveth you receiveth Me, and he that receiveth Me receiveth Him That sent Me.
Mt 10:41	He that receiveth a prophet in the name of a prophet shall receive a prophet's reward: and he that receiveth a righteous man in the name of a righteous man shall receive a righteous man's reward.
Mt 10:42	And whosoever shall give to drink unto one of these little ones a cup of cold water only in the name of a disciple, verily I say unto you, he shall in no wise lose his reward.
Mt 11:4	Go and shew John again those things which ye do hear and see:
Mt 11:5	The blind receive their sight and the lame walk, the lepers are cleansed and the deaf hear, the dead are raised up and the poor have the gospel preached to them.

Mt 11:6	And blessed is he, whosoever shall not be offended in Me.
Mt 11:7	What went ye out into the wilderness to see? A reed shaken with the wind?
Mt 11:8	But what went ye out for to see? A man clothed in soft raiment? Behold, they that wear soft clothing are in kings houses.
Mt 11:9	But what went ye out for to see? A prophet? Yea, I say unto you and more than a prophet.
Mt 11:10	For this is he, of whom it is written, Behold, I send My messenger before Thy face, which shall prepare Thy way before Thee.
Mt 11:11	Verily I say unto you, Among them that are born of women there hath not risen a greater than John, the Baptist; notwithstanding he that is least in the kingdom of heaven is greater than he.
Mt 11:12	And from the days of John the Baptist until now the kingdom of heaven suffereth violence and the violent take it by force.
Mt 11:13	For all the prophets and the law prophesied until John.
Mt 11:14	And if ye will receive it, this is Elias, which was for to come.
Mt 11:15	He that hath ears to hear, let him hear.

Mt 11:16 But whereunto shall I liken this generation? It is like unto children sitting in the markets, and calling unto their fellows.

Mt 11:17 And saying, We have piped unto you, and ye have not danced; we have mourned unto you and ye have not lamented.

Mt 11:18 For John came neither eating nor drinking and they say, He hath a devil.

Mt 11:19 The Son of man came eating and drinking and they say, Behold a man gluttonous and a winebibber, a friend of publicans and sinners. But Wisdom is justified of her children.

Mt 11:21 Woe unto thee, Chorazin! Woe unto thee, Bethsaida! For if the mighty works which were done in you, had been done in Tyre and Sidon, they would have repented long ago in sackcloth and ashes.

Mt 11:22 But I say unto you, It shall be more tolerable for Tyre and Sidon at the day of judgment, than for you.

Mt 11:23 And thou, Capernaum, which art exalted unto heaven, shalt be brought down to hell: for if the mighty works, which have been done in thee, had been done in Sodom, it would have remained until this day.

Mt 11:24	But I say unto you, That it shall be more tolerable for the land of Sodom in the day of judgment, than for thee.
Mt 11:25	I thank Thee, O Father, Lord of heaven and earth, because Thou hast hid these things from the wise and prudent, and hast revealed them unto babes.
Mt 11:26	Even so, Father: for so it seemed good in Thy sight.
Mt 11:27	All things are delivered unto Me of My Father: and no man knoweth the Son, but the Father; neither knoweth any man the Father, save the Son, and he to whomsoever the Son will reveal Him.
Mt 11:28	Come unto Me, all ye that labour and are heavy laden, and I will give you rest.
Mt 11:29	Take My yoke upon you and learn of Me; for I am meek and lowly in heart: and ye shall find rest unto your souls.
Mt 11:30	For My yoke is easy and My burden is light.
Mt 12:1	At that time Jesus went on the Sabbath day through the corn; and his disciples were an hungred and began to pluck the ears of corn, and to eat.

Mt 12:2	But when the pharisees saw it, they said unto him, Behold, thy disciples do that which is not lawful to do upon the Sabbath day.
Mt 12:3	Have ye not read what David did when he was an hundred and they were with him?
Mt 12:4	How he entered into the house of God, and did eat the shewbread, which was not lawful for him to eat, neither for them which were with him, but only for the priests?
Mt 12:5	Or have ye not read in the law, how that on the Sabbath days the priests in the temple profane the Sabbath and are blameless?
Mt 12:6	But I say unto you, That in this place is One greater than the temple.
Mt 12:7	But if ye had known what this meaneth, I will have mercy and not sacrifice, ye would not have condemned the guiltless.
Mt 12:8	For the Son of man is Lord even of the Sabbath day.
Mt 12:10	And, behold there was a man which had his hand withered. And they asked Him saying, Is it lawful to heal on the Sabbath days?
Mt 12:11	What man shall there be among you, that shall have one sheep and if it fall into a pit on the

	Sabbath day, will he not lay hold on it, and lift it out?
Mt 12:12	How much then is a man better than a sheep? Wherefore it is lawful to do well on the sabbath days.
Mt 12:13	Stretch forth thine hand. And he stretched it forth: and it was restored whole, like as the other.
Mt 12:18	Behold My Servant, Whom I have chosen: My Beloved, in Whom My soul is well pleased: I will put My spirit upon Him and He shall shew judgment to the Gentiles.
Mt 12:19	He shall not strive, nor cry; neither shall any man hear His voice in the streets.
Mt 12:20	A bruised reed shall He not break and smoking flax shall He not quench, till He send forth judgment unto victory.
Mt 12:21	And in His name shall the Gentiles trust.
Mt 12:25	Every kingdom divided against itself is brought to desolation; and every city or house divided against itself shall not stand:
Mt 12:26	And if Satan cast out Satan, he is divided against himself; how shall then his kingdom stand?

Mt 12:27   And if I by Beelzebub cast out devils, by whom
            do your children cast them out? Therefore they
            shall be your judges.

Mt 12:28   But if I cast out devils by the Spirit of God,
            then the kingdom of God is come unto you.

Mt 12:29   Or else how can one enter into a strong man's
            house and spoil his goods, except he first bind
            the strong man? And then he will spoil his
            house.

Mt 12:30   He that is not with Me is against Me; and he
            that gathereth not with Me scattereth abroad.

Mt 12:31   Wherefore I say unto you, All manner of sin
            and blasphemy shall be forgiven unto men: but
            the blasphemy against the Holy Ghost shall not
            be forgiven unto men.

Mt 12:32   And whosoever speaketh a word against the
            Son of man, it shall be forgiven him: but
            whosoever speaketh against the Holy Ghost, it
            shall not be forgiven him, neither in this world,
            neither in the world to come.

Mt 12:33   Either make the tree good and his fruit good; or
            else make the tree corrupt and his fruit corrupt:
            for the tree is known by his fruit.

Mt 12:34	O generation of vipers, how can ye, being evil, speak good things? For out of the abundance of the heart the mouth speaketh.
Mt 12:35	A good man out of the good treasure of the heart bringeth forth good things: and an evil man out of the evil treasure bringeth forth evil things.
Mt 12:36	But I say unto you, That every idle word that men shall speak, they shall give account thereof in the day of judgment.
Mt 12:37	For by thy words thou shalt be justified, and by thy words thou shalt be condemned.
Mt 12:38	Then certain of the scribes and of the Pharisees answered, saying, Master, we would see a sign from Thee.
Mt 12:39	An evil and adulterous generation seeketh after a sign; and there shall no sign be given to it, but the sign of the prophet Jonas:
Mt 12:40	For as Jonas was three days and three nights in the whale's belly; so shall the Son of man be three days and three nights in the heart of the earth.
Mt 12:41	The men of Nineveh shall rise in judgment with this generation and shall condemn it: because

	they repented at the preaching of Jonas; and behold, a greater than Jonas is here.
Mt 12:42	The queen of the south shall rise up in the judgment with this generation and shall condemn it; for she came from the uttermost parts of the earth to hear the wisdom of Solomon; and behold a greater than Solomon is here.
Mt 12:43	When the unclean spirit is gone out of a man, he walketh through dry places, seeking rest, and findeth none.
Mt 12:44	Then he saith, I will return into my house from whence I came out; and when he is come, he findeth it empty, swept and garnished.
Mt 12:45	Then goeth he, and taketh with himself seven other spirits more wicked than himself and they enter in and dwell there: and the last state of that man is worse than the first. Even so shall it be also unto this wicked generation.
Mt 12:48	Who is My mother? And who are My brethren?
Mt 12:49	Behold My mother and My brethren!
Mt 12:50	For whosoever shall do the will of My Father Which is in heaven, the same is My brother and sister and mother.

Mt 13:3	Behold, a sower went forth to sow;
Mt 13:4	And when he sowed, some seeds fell by the way side and the fowls came and devoured them up:
Mt 13:5	Some fell upon stony places, where they had not much earth: and forthwith thcy sprung up, because they had no deepness of earth:
Mt 13:6	And when the sun was up, they were scorched; and because they had no root, they withered away.
Mt 13:7	And some fell among thorns; and the thorns sprung up and choked them:
Mt 13:8	But other fell into good ground and brought forth fruit, some an hundredfold, some sixtyfold, some thirtyfold.
Mt 13:9	Who hath ears to hear, let him hear.
Mt 13:11	Because it is given unto you to know the mysteries of the kingdom of heaven, but to them it is not given.
Mt 13:12	For whosoever hath, to him shall be given, and he shall have more abundance: but whosoever hath not, from him shall be taken away even that he hath.

Mt 13:13	Therefore speak I to them in parables: because they seeing me not; and hearing they hear not, neither do they understand.
Mt 13:14	And in them is fulfilled the prophecy of Esaias, which saith, By hearing ye shall hear and shall not understand; and seeing ye shall see, and shall not perceive:
Mt 13:15	For this people's heart is waxed gross and their ears are dull of hearing and their eyes they have closed; lest at any time they should see with their eyes and hear with their ears and should understand with their heart and should be converted and I should heal them.
Mt 13:16	But blessed are your eyes for they see and your ears for they hear.
Mt 13:17	For verily I say unto you, That many prophets and righteous men have desired to see those things which ye see and have not seen them; and to hear those things which ye hear and have not heard them.
Mt 13:18	Hear ye therefore the parable of the sower.
Mt 13:19	When any one heareth the word of the kingdom and understandeth it not, then cometh the wicked one and catcheth away that which was

sown in his heart. This is he which received seed by the way side.

Mt 13:20   But he that received the seed into stony places, the same is he that heareth the word and anon, with joy receiveth it;

Mt 13:21   Yet hath he not root in himself, but dureth for a while; for when tribulation or persecution ariseth because of the word by and by he is offended.

Mt 13:22   He also that received seed among the thorns is he that heareth the word; and the care of this world and the deceitfulness of riches, choke the word and he becometh unfruitful.

Mt 13:23   But he that received seed into the good ground is he that heareth the word and understandeth it; which also beareth fruit and bringeth forth some an hundredfold, some sixty and some thirty.

Mt 13:24   The kingdom of heaven is likened unto a man which sowed good seed in his field:

Mt 13:25   But while men slept, his enemy came and sowed tares among the wheat and went his way.

Mt 13:26   But when the blade was sprung up and brought forth fruit, then appeared the tares also.

Mt 13:27	So the servants of the householder came and said unto him, Sir, didst not thou sow good seed in thy field? From whence then hath it tares?
Mt 13:28	He said unto them, An enemy hath done this.
Mt 13:29	Nay; lest while ye gather up the tares, ye root up also the wheat with them.
Mt 13:30	Let both grow together until the harvest; and in the time of harvest I will say to the reapers, Gather ye together first the tares, and bind them in bundles to burn them: but gather the wheat into my barn.
Mt 13:31	The kingdom of heaven is like to a grain of mustard seed, which a man took and sowed in his field:
Mt 13:32	Which indeed is the least of all seeds: but when it is grown, it is the greatest among herbs and becometh a tree so that the birds of the air come and lodge in the branches thereof.
Mt 13:33	The kingdom of heaven is like unto leaven, which a woman took and hid in three measures of meat, till the whole was leavened.
Mt 13:34	All these things spake Jesus unto the multitude in parables; and without a parable spake He not unto them:

Mt 13:35   I will open my mouth in parables; I will utter things which have been kept secret from the foundation of the world.

Mt 13:37   He that soweth the good seed is the Son of man;

Mt 13:38   The field is the world; the good seed are the children of the kingdom; but the tares are the children of the wicked one;

Mt 13:39   The enemy that sowed them is the devil; the harvest is the end of the world; and the reapers are the angels.

Mt 13:40   As therefore the tares are gathered and burned in the fire; so shall it be in the end of this world.

Mt 13:41   The Son of man shall send forth His angels and they shall gather out of His kingdom all things that offend and them which do iniquity;

Mt 13:42   And shall cast them into a furnace of fire: there shall be wailing and gnashing of teeth.

Mt 13:43   Then shall the righteous shine forth as the sun in the kingdom of their Father, Who hath ears to hear, let him hear.

Mt 13:44   Again, the kingdom of heaven is like unto treasure hid in a field; the which when a man hath found, he hideth and for joy thereof goeth

	and selleth all that he hath and buyeth that field.
Mt 13:45	Again, the kingdom of heaven is like unto a merchant man, seeking goodly pearls:
Mt 13:46	Who, when he had found one pearl of great price, went and sold all that he had and bought it.
Mt 13:47	Again, the kingdom of heaven is like unto a net, that was cast into the sea and gathered of every kind:
Mt 13:48	Which, when it was full, they drew to shore and sat down and gathered the good into vessels but cast the bad away.
Mt 13:49	So shall it be at the end of the world: the angels shall come forth and sever the wicked from among the just,
Mt 13:50	And shall cast them into the furnace of fire: there shall be wailing and gnashing of teeth.
Mt 13:51	Have ye understood all these things?
Mt 13:52	Therefore every scribe which is instructed unto the kingdom of heaven is like unto a man that is an householder, which bringeth forth out of his treasure things new and old.
Mt 13:54	And when He was come into His own country, He taught them in their synagogue, insomuch

that they were astonished, and He said, Whence hath this man this wisdom, and these mighty works?

Mt 13:57 And they were offended in Him. But Jesus said unto them, A prophet is not without honour, save in his own country and in his own house.

Mt 14:16 They need not depart; give ye them to eat.

Mt 14:18 Bring them hither to Me.

Mt 14:27 Be of good cheer; it is I; be not afraid.

Mt 14:31 O thou of little faith, wherefore didst thou doubt?

Mt 15:3 Why do ye also transgress the commandment of God by your tradition?

Mt 15:4 For God commanded, saying, Honour thy father and mother: and He that curseth father or mother, let him die the death.

Mt 15:5 But ye say, Whosoever shall say to his father or his mother, It is a gift, by whatsoever thou mightest be profited by me;

Mt 15:6 And honour not his father or his mother, he shall be free. Thus have ye made the commandment of God of none effect by your tradition.

Mt 15:7	Ye hypocrites, well did Esaias prophesy of you, saying,
Mt 15:8	This people draweth nigh unto Me with their mouth and honoureth Me with their lips; but their heart is far from Me.
Mt 15:9	But in vain they do worship Me, teaching for doctrines the commandments of men.
Mt 15:10	Hear and understand:
Mt 15:11	Not that which goeth into the mouth defileth a man; but that which cometh out of the mouth, this defileth a man.
Mt 15:13	Every plant, which My heavenly Father hath not planted, shall be rooted up.
Mt 15:14	Let them alone: they be blind leaders of the blind. And if the blind lead the blind, both shall fall into the ditch.
Mt 15:16	Are ye also yet without understanding?
Mt 15:17	Do not ye yet understand, that whatsoever entereth in at the mouth goeth into the belly and is cast out into the draught?
Mt 15:18	But those things which proceed out of the mouth come forth from the heart; and they defile the man.

Mt 15:19	For out of the heart proceed evil thoughts, murders, adulteries, fornications, thefts, false witness, blasphemies:
Mt 15:20	These are the things which defile a man: but to eat with unwashen hands defileth not a man.
Mt 15:22	And behold, a woman of Canaan came out of the same coasts, and cried unto Him, saying, have mercy on me, O Lord, thou Son of David; my daughter is grievously vexed with a devil.
Mt 15:24	I am not sent but unto the lost sheep of the house of Israel.
Mt 15:26	It is not meet to take the children's bread and to cast it to dogs.
Mt 15:28	O woman, great is thy faith: be it unto thee even as thou wilt.
Mt 15:32	I have compassion on the multitude because they continue with Me now three days and have nothing to eat: and I will not send them away fasting, lest they faint in the way.
Mt 15:34	How many loaves have ye?
Mt 16:2	When it is evening, ye say, It will be fair weather: for the sky is red.
Mt 16:3	And in the morning, It will be foul weather today: for the sky is red and lowring. O ye

	hypocrites, ye can discern the face of the sky; but can ye not discern the signs of the times?
Mt 16:4	A wicked and adulterous generation seeketh after a sign; and there shall no sign be given unto it, but the sign of the prophet Jonas.
Mt 16:6	Take heed and beware of the leaven of the Pharisees and of the Sadducees.
Mt 16:8	O ye of little faith, why reason ye among yourselves, because ye have brought no bread?
Mt 16:9	Do ye not yet understand, neither remember the five loaves of the five thousand and how many baskets ye took up?
Mt 16:10	Neither the seven loaves of the four thousand and how many baskets ye took up?
Mt 16:11	How is it that ye do not understand that I spake it not to you concerning bread, that ye should beware of the leaven of the Pharisees and of the Sadducees?
Mt 16:13	Whom do men say that I the Son of man am?
MT 16:15	But whom say ye that I am?
Mt 16:17	Blessed art thou, Simon Bar-jona: for flesh and blood hath not revealed it under thee, but My Father Which is in heaven.

Mt 16:18	And I say also unto thee, that Thou art Peter, and upon this rock I will build My church; and the gates of hell shall not prevail against it.
Mt 16:19	And I will give unto thee the keys of the kingdom of Heaven: and whatsoever thou shalt bind on earth shall be bound in heaven: and whatsoever thou shalt loose on earth shall be loosed in heaven.
Mt 16:23	Get thee behind Me, Satan: thou art in offence unto Me: for thou savourest not the things that be of God, but those that be of men.
Mt 16:24	If any man will come after Me, let him deny himself and take up his cross and follow Me.
Mt 16:25	For whosoever will save his life shall lose it: and whosoever will lose his life for My sake shall find it.
Mt 16:26	For what is a man profited, if he shall gain the whole world and lose his own soul? Or what shall a man give in exchange for his soul?
Mt 16:27	For the Son of man shall come in the glory of His Father with His angels; and then He shall reward every man according to his works.
Mt 16:28	Verily I say unto you, There be some standing here, which shall not taste of death, till they see the Son of man coming in His kingdom.

Mt 17:7	Arise and be not afraid.
Mt 17:8	And when they had lifted up their eyes, they saw no man, save Jesus only.
Mt 17:9	Tell the vision to no man, until the Son of man be risen again from the dead.
Mt 17:11	Elias truly shall first come and restore all things.
Mt 17:12	But I say unto you, That Elias is come already and they knew him not, but have done unto him whatsoever thy listed. Likewise shall also the Son of man suffer of them.
Mt 17:17	O faithless and perverse generation, how long shall I be with you? How long shall I suffer you? Bring him hither to Me.
Mt 17:20	Because of your unbelief: for verily I say unto you, If ye have faith as a grain of mustard seed, ye shall say unto this mountain, Remove hence to yonder place; and it shall remove; and nothing shall be impossible unto you.
Mt 17:21	Howbeit this kind goeth not out but by prayer and fasting.
Mt 17:22	The Son of man shall be betrayed into the hands of men:
Mt 17:23	And they shall kill Him and the third day He shall be raised again.

Mt 17:24   And when they were come to Capernaum, they that received tribute money came to Peter, and said, doth not your master pay tribute?

Mt 17:25   He saith, Yes. And when He was come into the house, Jesus prevented him, saying, What thinkest thou, Simon? Of whom do the kings of the earth take custom or tribute? Of their own children or of strangers?

Mt 17:26   Then are the children free.

Mt 17:27   Notwithstanding, lest we should offend them, go thou to the sea and cast an hook, and take up the fish that first cometh up; and when thou hast opened his mouth, thou shalt find a piece of money: that take and give unto them for Me and thee.

Mt 18:1   At the same time came the disciples unto Jesus, saying, Who is the greatest in the kingdom of heaven?

Mt 18:3   Verily I say unto you, Except ye be converted and become as little children, ye shall not enter into the kingdom of heaven.

Mt 18:4   Whosoever therefore shall humble himself as this little child, the same is greatest in the kingdom of heaven.

Mt 18:5	And whoso shall receive one such little child in My name receiveth Me.
Mt 18:6	But whoso shall offend one of these little ones which believe in Me, it were better for him that a millstone were hanged about his neck and that he were drowned in the depth of the sea.
Mt 18:7	Woe unto the world because of offences! For it must needs be that offences come; but woe to that man by whom the offence cometh!
Mt 18:8	Wherefore if thy hand or thy foot offend thee, cut them off and cast them from thee: it is better for thee to enter into life halt or maimed, rather than having two hands or two feet to be cast into everlasting fire.
Mt 18:9	And if thine eye offend thee, pluck it out and cast it from thee: it is better for thee to enter into life with one eye, rather than having two eyes to be cast into hell fire.
Mt 18:10	Take heed that ye despise not one of these little ones; for I say unto you, That in heaven their angels do always behold the face of My Father Which is in heaven.
Mt 18:11	For the Son of man is come to save that which was lost.

Mt 18:12	How think ye? If a man have an hundred sheep and one of them be gone astray, doth he not leave the ninety and nine and goeth into the mountains and seeketh that which is gone astray?
Mt 18:13	And if so be that he find it, verily I say unto you, he rejoiceth more of that sheep, than of the ninety and nine which went not astray.
Mt 18:14	Even so it is not the will of your Father Which is in heaven, that one of these little ones should perish.
Mt 18:15	Moreover if thy brother shall trespass against thee, go and tell him his fault between thee and him alone: if he shall hear thee, thou hast gained thy brother.
Mt 18:16	But if he will not hear thee, then take with thee one or two more, that in the mouth of two or three witnesses every word may be established.
Mt 18:17	And if he shall neglect to hear them, tell it unto the church: but if he neglect to hear the church, let him be unto thee as an heathen man and a publican.
Mt 18:18	Verily I say unto you, Whatsoever ye shall bind on earth shall be bound in heaven: and

whatsoever ye shall loose on earth shall be loosed in heaven.

Mt 18:19 Again I say unto you, That if two of you shall agree on earth as touching anything that they shall ask, it shall be done for them of My Father Which is in heaven.

Mt 18:20 For where two or three are gathered together in My name, there am I in the midst of them.

Mt 18:21 Then came Peter to him and said, Lord, how oft shall my brother sin against me and I forgive him? Till seven times?

Mt 18:22 I say not unto thee, Until seven times: but, Until seventy times seven.

Mt 18:23 Therefore is the kingdom of heaven likened unto a certain king, which would take account of his servants.

Mt 18:24 And when he had begun to reckon, one was brought unto him, which owed him ten thousand talents.

Mt 18:25 But forasmuch as he had not to pay, his lord commanded him to be sold, and his wife, and children, and all that he had and payment to be made.

Mt 18:26	The servant therefore fell down and worshipped him saying, lord, have patience with me and I will pay thee all.
Mt 18:27	Then the lord of that servant was moved with compassion and loosed him and forgave him the debt.
Mt 18:28	But the same servant went out and found one of his fellowservants which owed him an hundred pence: and he laid hands on him and took him by the throat saying, Pay me that thou owest.
Mt 18:29	And his fellowservant fell down at his feet and besought him, saying, Have patience with me and I will pay thee all.
Mt 18:30	And he would not: but went and cast him into prison till he should pay the debt.
Mt 18:31	So when his fellowservants saw what was done, they were very sorry and came and told unto their lord all that was done.
Mt 18:32	Then his lord, after that he had called him, said unto him O thou wicked servant, I forgave thee all that debt, because thou desiredst me:
Mt 18:33	Shouldest not thou also have had compassion on thy fellowservant, even as I had pity on thee?

Mt 18:34	And his lord was wroth and delivered him to the tormentors till he should pay all that was due unto him.
Mt 18:35	So likewise shall My heavenly Father do also unto you, if ye from your hearts forgive not every one his brother their trespasses.
Mt 19:4	Have ye not read that He Which made them at the beginning made them male and female.
Mt 19:5	For this cause shall a man leave father and mother and shall cleave to his wife: and they twain shall be one flesh?
Mt 19:6	Wherefore they are no more twain, but one flesh. What therefore God hath joined together, let not man put asunder.
Mt 19:8	Moses, because of the hardness of your hearts suffered you to put away your wives: but from the beginning it was not so.
Mt 19:9	Whosoever shall put away his wife, except it be for fornication, and shall marry another committeth adultery: and whoso marrieth her which is put away doth commit adultery.
Mt 19:11	All men cannot receive this saying save they to whom it is given.

Mt 19:12 For there are some eunuchs which were so born from their mothers womb: and there are some eunuchs which were made eunuchs of men: and there be eunuchs which have made themselves eunuchs for the kingdom of heavens sake. He that is able to receive it, let him receive it.

Mt 19:13 Then were there brought unto Him little children, that He should put His hands on them, and pray: and the disciples rebuked them.

Mt 19:14 Suffer little children, and forbid them not to come unto Me: for of such is the kingdom of heaven.

Mt 19:16 And, behold, one came and said unto Him, Good Master, what good thing shall I do, that I may have eternal life?

Mt 19:17 Why callest thou Me good? There is none good but One that is God: but if thou wilt enter into life, keep the commandments.

Mt 19:18 Thou shalt do no murder, Thou shalt not commit adultery, Thou shalt not steal, Thou shalt not bear false witness,

Mt 19:19 Honour thy father and thy mother; and Thou shalt love thy neighbour as thyself.

Mt 19:21	If thou wilt be perfect, go and sell that thou hast and give to the poor and thou shalt have treasure in heaven: and come and follow Me.
Mt 19:23	Verily I say unto you, That a rich man shall hardly enter into the kingdom of heaven.
Mt 19:24	And again I say unto you, It is easier for a camel to go through the eye of a needle, than for a rich man to enter into the kingdom of God.
Mt 19:26	With men this is impossible; but with God all things are possible.
Mt 19:28	Verily I say unto you, That ye which have followed Me, in the regeneration when the Son of man shall sit in the throne of His glory, ye also shall sit upon twelve thrones, judging the twelve tribes of Israel.
Mt 19:29	And every one that hath forsaken houses or brethren or sisters or father or mother or wife or children or lands for My name sake shall receive an hundredfold and shall inherit everlasting life.
Mt 19:30	But many that are first shall be last and the last shall be first.

Mt 20:1	For the kingdom of heaven is like unto a man that is an householder, which went out early in the morning to hire labourers into his vineyard.
Mt 20:2	And when he had agreed with the labourers for a penny a day, he sent them into his vineyard.
Mt 20:3	And he went out about the third hour and saw others standing idle in the marketplace.
Mt 20:4	And said unto them; Go ye also into the vineyard and whatsoever is right I will give you. And they went their way.
Mt 20:5	Again he went out about the sixth and ninth hour and did likewise.
Mt 20:6	And about the eleventh hour he went out and found others standing idle and saith unto them, Why stand ye here all the day idle?
Mt 20:7	They say unto him, Because no man hath hired us. He saith unto them, Go ye also into the vineyard and whatsoever is right, that shall ye receive.
Mt 20:8	So when even was come, the lord of the vineyard saith unto his steward, Call the labourers and give them their hire, beginning from the last unto the first.

Mt 20:9	And when they came that were hired about the eleventh hour, they received every man a penny.
Mt 20:10	But when the first came, they supposed that they should have received more; and they likewise received every man a penny.
Mt 20:11	And when they had received it, they murmured against the Goodman of the house
Mt 20:12	Saying, These last have wrought but one hour and thou hast made them equal unto us, which have borne the burden and heat of the day.
Mt 20:13	But he answered one of them and said Friend, I do thee no wrong; didst not thou agree with me for a penny?
Mt 20:14	Take that thine is and go thy way: I will give unto this last, even as unto thee.
Mt 20:15	Is it not lawful for me to do what I will with mine own? Is thine eye evil because I am good?
Mt 20:16	So the last shall be first and the first last; for many be called, but few chosen.
Mt 20:18	Behold, we go up to Jerusalem; and the Son of man shall be betrayed unto the chief priests and unto the scribes and they shall condemn Him to death,

Mt 20:19 And shall deliver Him to the Gentiles to mock and to scourge and to crucify Him; and the third day He shall rise again.

Mt 20:20 Then came to him the mother of Zebedee's children with her sons, worshipping him and desiring a certain thing of him.

Mt 20:21 And he said unto her, What wilt thou? She saith unto him, Grant that these my two sons may sit, the one on thy right hand and the other on the left in thy kingdom.

Mt 20:22 Ye know not what ye ask. Are ye able to drink of the cup that I shall drink of and to be baptized with the baptism that I am baptized with? They say unto him, We are able.

Mt 20:23 Ye shall drink indeed of My cup and be baptized with the baptism that I am baptized with: but to sit on My right hand and on My left is not Mine to give, but it shall be given to them for whom it is prepared of My Father.

Mt 20:25 Ye know that the princes of the Gentiles exercise dominion over them and they that are great exercise authority upon them.

Mt 20:26 But it shall not be so among you: but whosoever will be great among you, let him be your minister;

Mt 20:27   And whosoever will be chief among you, let him be your servant:

Mt 20:28   Even as the Son of man came not to be ministered unto but to minister and to give His life a ransom for many.

Mt 20:30   And, behold, two blind men sitting by the way side, when they heard that Jesus passed by, cried out, saying Have mercy on us, O Lord, thou son of David.

Mt 20:32   What will ye that I shall do unto you?

Mt 20:34   So Jesus had compassion on them and touched their eyes: and immediately their eyes received sight and they followed him.

Mt 21:2   Go into the village over against you and straightway ye shall find an ass tied and a colt with her: loose them and bring them unto Me.

Mt 21:3   And if any man say ought unto you, ye shall say, The Lord hath need of them and straightway he will send them.

Mt 21:12   And Jesus went into the temple of God and cast out all them that sold and bought in the temple and overthrew the tables of the moneychangers and the seats of them that sold doves.

Mt 21:13	It is written, My house shall be called the house of prayer; but ye have made it a den of thieves.
Mt 21:15	And when the chief priests and scribes saw the wonderful things that He did and the children crying in the temple and saying, Hosanna to the Son of David: they were sore displeased,
Mt 21:16	Yea: have ye never read, Out of the mouth of babes and sucklings Thou hast perfected praise?
Mt 21:19	Let no fruit grow on thee henceforward for ever.
Mt 21:21	Verily I say unto you, If ye have faith and doubt not, ye shall not only do this which is done to the fig tree, but also if ye shall say unto this mountain. Be thou removed and be thou cast into the sea; it shall be done.
Mt 21:22	And all things whatsoever ye shall ask in prayer, believing, ye shall receive.
Mt 21:23	And when he was come into the temple, the chief priests and the elders of the people came unto him as he was teaching and said, By what authority doest thou these things? And who gave thee this authority?

Mt 21:24	I also will ask you one thing, which if ye tell Me, I in like wise will tell you by what authority I do these things.
Mt 21:25	The baptism of John, whence was it? From heaven or of men? And they reasoned with themselves, saying, If we shall say, From heaven: he will say unto us, Why did ye not then believe him?
Mt 21:26	But if we shall say, Of men; we fear the people; for all hold John as a prophet.
Mt 21:27	And they answered Jesus, and said, We cannot tell. And he said unto them, Neither tell I you by what authority I do these things.
Mt 21:28	But what think ye? A certain man had two sons and he came to the first and said, Son, go work today in my vineyard.
Mt 21:29	He answered and said, I will not: but afterward he repented and went.
Mt 21:30	And he came to the second and said likewise. And he answered and said, I go sir; and went not.
Mt 21:31	Whether of them twain did the will of his father? They say unto him, The first. Verily I say unto you, That the publicans and the harlots go into the kingdom of God before you.

Mt 21:32	For John came unto you in the way of righteousness and ye believed him not; but the publicans and the harlots believed him? And ye, when ye had seen it, repented not afterward that ye might believe him.
Mt 21:33	Hear another parable: There was a certain householder which planted a vineyard and hedged it round about and digged a winepress in it and built a tower and let it out to husbandmen and went into a far country:
Mt 21:34	And when the time of the fruit drew near, he sent his servants to the husbandmen that they might receive the fruits of it.
Mt 21:35	And the husbandmen took his servants and beat one and killed another and stoned another.
Mt 21:36	Again he sent other servants more than the first: and they did unto them likewise.
Mt 21:37	But last of all he sent unto them his son saying, They will reverence my son.
Mt 21:38	But when the husbandmen saw the Son, they said among themselves, This is the heir; come, let us kill him and let us seize on his inheritance.
Mt 21:39	And they caught him and cast him out of the vineyard and slew him.

Mt 21:40   When the lord therefore of the vineyard
            cometh, what will he do unto those
            husbandmen?

Mt 21:41   They say unto him, He will miserably destroy
            those wicked men and will let out his vineyard
            unto other husbandmen, which shall render him
            the fruits in their seasons.

Mt 21:42   Did ye never read in the scriptures. The stone
            which the builders rejected, the same is become
            the head of the corner: this is the Lord's doing
            and it is marvelous in our eyes?

Mt 21:43   Therefore say I unto you, The kingdom of God
            shall be taken from you and given to a nation
            bringing forth the fruits thereof.

Mt 21:44   And whosoever shall fall on this Stone shall be
            broken: but on whomsoever It shall fall, It will
            grind him to powder.

Mt 22:2   The kingdom of heaven is like unto a certain
            king which made a marriage for his son,

Mt 22:3   And sent forth his servants to call them that
            were bidden to the wedding: and they would
            not come.

Mt 22:4   Again he sent forth other servants, saying, Tell
            them which are bidden, Behold I have prepared

my dinner: my oxen and my fatlings are killed and all things are ready: come unto the marriage.

Mt 22:5 But they made light of it and went their ways one to his farm, another to his merchandise:

Mt 22:6 And the remnant took his servants and entreated them spitefully and slew them.

Mt 22:7 But when the king heard thereof, he was wroth; and he sent forth his armies and destroyed those murderers and burned up their city.

Mt 22:8 Then saith he to his servants, The wedding is ready, but they which were bidden were not worthy.

Mt 22:9 Go ye therefore into the highways and as many as ye shall find, bid to the marriage.

Mt 22:10 So those servants went out into the highways and gathered together all as many as they found, both bad and good: and the wedding was furnished with guests.

Mt 22:11 And when the king came in to see the guests, he saw there a man which had not on a wedding garment:

Mt 22:12 And he saith unto him, Friend, how camest thou in hither not having a wedding garment? And he was speechless.

Mt 22:13   Then said the king to the servants, Bind him hand and foot and take him away and cast him into outer darkness; there shall be weeping and gnashing of teeth.

Mt 22:14   For many are called, but few are chosen.

Mt 22:18   Why tempt ye Me, ye hypocrites?

Mt 22:19   Shew Me the tribute money. And they brought unto Him a penny.

Mt 22:20   Whose is this image and superscription?

Mt 22:21   Render therefore unto Caesar the things which are Caesar's; and unto God the things that are God's.

Mt 22:25   Now there were with us seven brethren: and the first, when he had married a wife, deceased and having no issue, left his wife unto his brother:

Mt 22:29   Ye do err, not knowing the scriptures, nor the power of God.

Mt 22:30   For in the resurrection they neither marry, nor are given in marriage, but are as the angels of God in heaven.

Mt 22:31   But as touching the resurrection of the dead, have ye not read that which was spoken unto you by God, saying.

Mt 22:32	I am the God of Abraham and the God of Isaac and the God of Jacob.
	God is not the God of the dead but of the living.
Mt 22:37	Thou shalt love the Lord thy God with all thy heart and with all thy soul and with all thy mind.
Mt 22:38	This is the first and great commandment,
Mt 22:39	And the second is like unto it, Thou shalt love thy neighbour as thyself.
Mt 22:40	On these two commandments hang all the law and the prophets.
Mt 22:42	What think ye of Christ? Whose Son is He? They say unto him, The son of David.
Mt 22:43	How then doth David in spirit call him Lord saying,
Mt 22:44	The Lord said unto My Lord, Sit Thou on My right hand, till I make Thine enemies Thy footstool?
Mt 22:45	If David then call Him Lord, how is He his Son?
Mt 22:46	And no man was able to answer him a word, neither durst any man from that day forth ask him any more questions.

Mt 23:2	The scribes and the Pharisees sit in Moses seat:
Mt 23:3	All therefore whatsoever they bid you observe, that observe and do: but do not ye after their works: for they say and do not.
Mt 23:4	For they bind heavy burdens, and grievous to be borne, and lay them on men's shoulders; but they themselves will not move them, with one of their fingers.
Mt 23:5	But all their works they do for to be seen of men: they make broad their phylacteries and enlarge the borders of their garments.
Mt 23:6	And love the uppermost rooms at feasts and the chief seats in the synagogues.
Mt 23:7	And greetings in the markets and to be called of men, Rabbi, Rabbi.
Mt 23:8	But be not ye called Rabbi: for One is your Master, even Christ; and all ye are brethren.
Mt 23:9	And call no man your father upon the earth: for One is your Father, Which is in heaven.
Mt 23:10	Neither be ye called masters: for One is your Master, even Christ.
Mt 23:11	But he that is greatest among you shall be your servant.

Mt 23:12   And whosoever shall exalt himself shall be
               abased; and he that shall humble himself shall
               be exalted.

Mt 23:13   But woe unto you scribes and Pharisees,
               hypocrites! For ye shut up the kingdom of
               heaven against men: for ye neither go in
               yourselves, neither suffer ye them that are
               entering to go in.

Mt 23:14   Woe unto you scribes and Pharisees,
               hypocrites! For ye devour widows houses and
               for a pretence make long prayer: therefore ye
               shall receive the greater damnation.

Mt 23:15   Woe unto you scribes and Pharisees,
               hypocrites! For ye compass sea and land to
               make one proselyte and when he is made, ye
               make him twofold more the child of hell than
               yourselves.

Mt 23:16   Woe unto you, ye blind guides, which say,
               Whosoever shall swear by the Temple, it is
               nothing: but whosoever shall swear by the gold
               of the Temple, he is a debtor!

Mt 23:17   Ye fools and blind: for whether is greater, the
               gold or the Temple that sanctifieth the gold?

Mt 23:18   And, Whosoever shall swear by the altar, it is nothing; but whosoever sweareth by the gift that is upon it, he is guilty.

Mt 23:19   Ye fools and blind: for whether is greater, the gift or the altar that sanctifieth the gift?

Mt 23:20   Whoso therefore shall swear by the altar, sweareth by it and by all things thereon.

Mt 23:21   And whoso shall swear by the Temple, sweareth by it and by Him That dwelleth therein.

Mt 23:22   And he that shall swear by heaven, sweareth by the throne of God and by Him That sitteth thereon.

Mt 23:23   Woe unto you, scribes and Pharisees, hypocrites! For ye pay tithe of mint and anise and cummin and have omitted the weightier matters of the law, judgment, mercy, and faith: these ought ye to have done and not to leave the other undone.

Mt 23:24   Ye blind guides, which strain at a gnat and swallow a camel.

Mt 23:25   Woe unto you, scribes and Pharisees, hypocrites! For ye make clean the outside of the cup, and of the platter, but within they are full of extortion and excess.

Mt 23:26	Thou blind Pharisee, cleanse first that which is within the cup and platter, that the outside of them may be clean also.
Mt 23:27	Woe unto you, scribes and Pharisees, hypocrites! for ye are like unto whited sepulchres which indeed appear beautiful outward, but are within full of dead men's bones, and of all uncleanness.
Mt 23:28	Even so ye also outwardly appear righteous unto men, but within ye are full of hypocrisy and iniquity.
Mt 23:29	Woe unto you, scribes and Pharisees, hypocrites! Because ye build the tombs of the prophets and garnish the sepulchres of the righteous.
Mt 23:30	And say, If we had been in the days of our fathers, we would not have been partakers with them in the blood of the prophets.
Mt 23:31	Wherefore ye be witnesses unto yourselves, that ye are the children of them which killed the prophets.
Mt 23:32	Fill ye up then the measure of your fathers.
Mt 23:33	Ye serpents, ye generation of vipers, how can ye escape the damnation of hell?

Mt 23:34	Wherefore, behold, I send unto you prophets and wise men and scribes: and some of them ye shall kill and crucify; and some of them shall ye scourge in your synagogues and persecute them from city to city:
Mt 23:35	That upon you may come all the righteous blood shed upon the earth, from the blood of righteous Abel unto the blood of Zacharias son of Barachias, whom ye slew between the Temple and the altar.
Mt 23:36	Verily I say unto you, All these things shall come upon this generation.
Mt 23:37	O Jerusalem, Jerusalem, thou that killest the prophets and stonest them which are sent unto thee, how often would I have gathered thy children together, even as a hen gathereth her chickens under her wings and ye would not!
Mt 23:38	Behold, your house is left unto you desolate.
Mt 23:39	For I say unto you, Ye shall not see Me henceforth, till ye shall say, Blessed is He That cometh in the name of the Lord.
Mt 24:2	See ye not all these things? Verily I say unto you, There shall not be left here one stone upon another, that shall not be thrown down.

Mt 24:4	Take heed that no man deceive you.
Mt 24:5	For many shall come in My name, saying, I am Christ; and shall deceive many.
Mt 24:6	And ye shall hear of wars and rumours of wars: see that ye be not troubled: for all these things must come to pass but the end is not yet.
Mt 24:7	For nation shall rise against nation and kingdom against kingdom and there shall be famines and pestilences and earthquakes in divers places.
Mt 24:8	All these are the beginning of sorrows.
Mt 24:9	Then shall they deliver you up to be afflicted and shall kill you: and ye shall be hated of all nations for My name's sake.
Mt 24:10	And then shall many be offended and shall betray one another and shall hate one another.
Mt 24:11	And many false prophets shall rise, and shall deceive many.
Mt 24:12	And because iniquity shall abound, the love of many shall wax cold.
Mt 24:13	But he that shall endure unto the end, the same shall be saved.
Mt 24:14	And this gospel of the kingdom shall be preached in all the world for a witness unto all nations; and then shall the end come.

Mt 24:15	When ye therefore shall see the abomination of desolation, spoken of by Daniel the prophet, stand in the holy place, (whoso readeth, let him understand:)
Mt 24:16	Then let them which be in Judaea flee into the mountains:
Mt 24:17	Let him which is on the housetop not come down to take any thing out of his house:
Mt 24:18	Neither let him which is in the field return back to take his clothes.
Mt 24:19	And woe unto them that are with child, and to them that give suck in those days!
Mt 24:20	But pray ye that your flight be not in the winter, neither on the Sabbath day:
Mt 24:21	For then shall be great tribulation, such as was not since the beginning of the world to this time, no, nor ever shall be.
Mt 24:22	And except those days should be shortened, there should no flesh be saved; but for the elect's sake those days shall be shortened.
Mt 24:23	Then if any man shall say unto you, Lo, here is Christ, or there; believe it not.
Mt 24:24	For there shall arise false Christs and false prophets and shall shew great signs and

wonders: insomuch that if it were possible, they shall deceive the very elect.

Mt 24:25 Behold, I have told you before,

Mt 24:26 Wherefore if they shall say unto you, Behold, He is in the desert; go not forth: behold He is in the secret chambers; believe it not.

Mt 24:27 For as the lightning cometh out of the east and shineth even unto the west; so shall also the coming of the Son of man be.

Mt 24:28 For wheresoever the carcase is, there will the eagles be gathered together.

Mt 24:29 Immediately after the tribulation of those days shall the sun be darkened and the moon shall not give her light and the stars shall fall from heaven and the powers of the heavens shall be shaken:

Mt 24:30 And then shall appear the sign of the Son of man in heaven: and then shall all the tribes of the earth mourn, and they shall see the Son of man coming in the clouds of heaven with power and great glory.

Mt 24:31 And He shall send His angels with a great sound of a trumpet and they shall gather together His elect from the four winds from one end of heaven to the other.

Mt 24:32   Now learn a parable of the fig tree; When his branch is yet tender and putteth forth leaves, ye know that summer is nigh:

Mt 24:33   So likewise ye, when ye shall see all these things, know that it is near, even at the doors.

Mt 24:34   Verily I say unto you, This generation shall not pass, till all these things be fulfilled.

Mt 24:35   Heaven and earth shall pass away, but My words shall not pass away.

Mt 24:36   But of that day and hour knoweth no man, no, not the angels of heaven, but My Father only.

Mt 24:37   But as the days of Noe were, so shall also the coming of the Son of man be.

Mt 24:38   For as in the days that were before the flood they were eating and drinking, marrying and giving in marriage, until the day that Noe entered into the ark,

Mt 24:39   And knew not until the flood came and took them all away; so shall also the coming of the Son of man be.

Mt 24:40   Then shall two be in the field; the one shall be taken and the other left.

Mt 24:41   Two women shall be grinding at the mill; the one shall be taken and the other left.

Mt 24:42	Watch therefore: for ye know not what hour your Lord doth come.
Mt 24:43	But know this, that if the Goodman of the house had known in what watch the thief would come, he would have watched and would not have suffered his house to be broken up.
Mt 24:44	Therefore be ye also ready: for in such an hour as ye think not the Son of man cometh.
Mt 24:45	Who then is a faithful and wise servant, whom his lord hath made ruler over his household, to give them meat in due season?
Mt 24:46	Blessed is that servant, whom his lord when he cometh shall find so doing.
Mt 24:47	Verily I say unto you, That he shall make him ruler over all his goods.
Mt 24:48	But and if that evil servant shall say in his heart, My lord delayeth his coming;
Mt 24:49	And shall begin to smite his fellowservants and to eat and drink with the drunken;
Mt 24:50	The lord of that servant shall come in a day when he looketh not for him and in an hour that he is not aware of,
Mt 24:51	And shall cut him asunder and appoint him his portion with the hypocrites: there shall be weeping and gnashing of teeth.

Mt 25:1   Then shall the kingdom of heaven be likened
            unto ten virgins which took their lamps and
            went forth to meet the bridegroom.

Mt 25:2   And five of them were wise and five were
            foolish.

Mt 25:3   They that were foolish took their lamps and
            took no oil with them:

Mt 25:4   But the wise took oil in their vessels with their
            lamps.

Mt 25:5   While the bridegroom tarried, they all
            slumbered and slept.

Mt 25:6   And at midnight there was a cry made, Behold,
            the bridegroom cometh; go ye out to meet him.

Mt 25:7   Then all those virgins arose and trimmed their
            lamps.

Mt 25:8   And the foolish said unto the wise, Give us of
            your oil; for our lamps are gone out.

Mt 25:9   But the wise answered saying, Not so; lest there
            be not enough for us and you: but go ye rather
            to them that sell and buy for yourselves.

Mt 25:10   And while they went to buy the bridegroom
            came; and they that were ready went in with
            him to the marriage: and the door was shut.

Mt 25:11	Afterward came also the other virgins, saying, lord, lord, open to us.
Mt 25:12	But he answered and said, Verily I say unto you, I know you not.
Mt 25:13	Watch therefore, for ye know neither the day nor the hour wherein the Son of man cometh.
Mt 25:14	For the kingdom of heaven is as a man traveling into a far country, who called his own servants and delivered unto them his goods.
Mt 25:15	And unto one he gave five talents to another two, and to another one; to every man according to his several ability; and straightway took his journey.
Mt 25:16	Then he that had received the five talents went and traded with the same and made them other five talents.
Mt 25:17	And likewise he that had received two he also gained other two.
Mt 25:18	But he that had received one went and digged in the earth and hid his lord's money.
Mt 25:19	After a long time the lord of those servants cometh and reckoneth with them.
Mt 25:20	And so he that had received five talents came and brought other five talents, saying, Lord,

thou deliveredst unto me five talents: behold I have gained beside them five talents more.

Mt 25:21 His lord said unto him, Well done, thou good and faithful servant: thou hast been faithful over a few things, I will make thee ruler over many things; enter thou into the joy of the lord.

Mt 25:22 He also that had received two talents came and said, Lord, thou deliveredst unto me two talents: behold, I have gained two other talents beside them.

Mt 25:23 His lord said unto him, Well done, good and faithful servant; thou hast been faithful over a few things I will make thee ruler over many things: enter thou into the joy of the lord.

Mt 25:24 Then he which had received the one talent came and said lord, I knew thee that thou art an hard man reaping where thou hast not sown, and gathering where thou hast not strawed:

Mt 25:25 And I was afraid, and went and hid thy talent in the earth: lo there thou hast that is thine.

Mt 25:26 His lord answered and said unto him, Thou wicked and slothful servant, thou knowest that I reap where I sowed not, and gather where I have not strawed:

Mt 25:27   Thou oughtest therefore to have put my money to the exchangers and then at my coming I should have received mine own with usury.

Mt 25:28   Take therefore the talent from him, and give it unto him which hath ten talents.

Mt 25:29   For unto every one that hath shall be given and he shall have abundance: but from him that hath not shall be taken away even that which he hath.

Mt 25:30   And cast ye the unprofitable servant into outer darkness: there shall be weeping and gnashing of teeth.

Mt 25:31   When the Son of man shall come in His glory and all the holy angels with Him then shall He sit upon the throne of His glory:

Mt 25:32   And before Him shall be gathered all nations: and He shall separate them one from another, as a shepherd divideth his sheep from the goats:

Mt 25:33   And He shall set the sheep on His right hand, but the goats on the left.

Mt 25:34   Then shall the King say unto them on His right hand, Come, ye blessed of My Father, inherit the kingdom prepared for you from the foundation of the world:

Mt 25:35	For I was an hungred and ye gave Me meat: I was thirsty and ye gave Me drink: I was a stranger and ye took Me in:
Mt 25:36	Naked and ye clothed Me: I was sick an ye visited Me: I was in prison and ye came unto Me.
Mt 25:37	Then shall the righteous answer Him, saying, Lord, when saw we Thee an hungred and fed Thee? Or thirsty and gave Thee drink?
Mt 25:38	When saw we Thee a stranger and took Thee in? Or naked and clothed Thee?
Mt 25:39	Or when saw we Thee sick, or in prison, and came unto Thee?
Mt 25:40	And the King shall answer and say unto them Verily I say unto you, Inasmuch as ye have done it unto one of the least of these My brethren, ye have done it unto Me.
Mt 25:41	Then shall He say also unto them on the left hand, Depart from Me, ye cursed, into everlasting fire, prepared for the devil and his angels:
Mt 25:42	For I was an hungred and ye gave Me no meat: I was thirsty and ye gave Me no drink:

Mt 25:43   I was a stranger and ye took Me not in; naked and ye clothed Me not: sick and in prison and ye visited Me not.

Mt 25:44   Then shall they also answer Him, saying, lord, when saw we Thee an hungred, or a thirst, or a stranger or naked or sick or in prison and did not minister unto Thee?

Mt 25:45   Then shall He answer them, saying, Verily I say unto you, inasmuch as ye did not to one of the least of these, ye did it not to Me.

Mt 25:46   And these shall go away into everlasting punishment: but the righteous into life eternal.

Mt 26:2   Ye know that after two days is the feast of the Passover and the Son of man is betrayed to be crucified.

Mt 26:7   There came unto him a woman having an alabaster box of very precious ointment and poured it on his head, as he sat at meat.

Mt 26:8   But when his disciples saw it they had indignation, saying, To what purpose is this waste?

Mt 26:9   For this ointment might have been sold for much and given to the poor.

Mt 26:10	Why trouble ye the woman? For she hath wrought a good work upon Me.
Mt 26:11	For ye have the poor always with you; but Me ye have not always.
Mt 26:12	For in that she hath poured this ointment on My body, she did it for My burial.
Mt 26:13	Verily I say unto you, Wheresoever this gospel shall be preached in the whole world, there shall also this, that this woman hath done, be told for a memorial of her.
Mt 26:18	Go into the city to such a man and say unto him, The Master saith, My time is at hand; I will keep the Passover at thy house with My disciples.
Mt 26:21	Verily I say unto you that one of you shall betray Me.
Mt 26:23	He that dippeth his hand with Me in the dish, the same shall betray Me.
Mt 26:24	The Son of man goeth as it is written of Him: but woe unto that man by whom the Son of man is betrayed! It had been good for that man if he had not been born.
Mt 26:26	Take, eat; this is My body.
Mt 26:27	Drink ye all of it:

Mt 26:28   For this is My blood of the new testament, which is shed for many for the remission of sins.

Mt 26:29   But I say unto you, I will not drink henceforth of this fruit of the vine until that day when I drink it new with you in My Father's kingdom.

Mt 26:31   All ye shall be offended because of Me this night: for it is written, I will smite the shepherd and the sheep of the flock shall be scattered abroad.

Mt 26:32   But after I am risen again, I will go before you into Galilee.

Mt 26:34   Verily I say unto thee, That this night, before the cock crow, thou shalt deny Me thrice.

Mt 26:36   Sit ye here while I go and pray yonder.

Mt 26:38   My soul is exceeding sorrowful, even unto death: tarry ye here and watch with Me.

Mt 26:39   O My Father, if it be possible, let this cup pass from Me: nevertheless not as I will, but as Thou wilt.

Mt 26:40   What could ye not watch with Me one hour?

Mt 26:41   Watch and pray, that ye enter not into temptation: the spirit indeed is willing, but the flesh is weak.

Mt 26:42	O My Father, if this cup may not pass away from Me, except I drink it, Thy will be done.
Mt 26:45	Sleep on now and take your rest: behold, the hour is at hand and the Son of man is betrayed into the hands of sinners.
Mt 26:46	Rise, let us be going: behold, he is at hand that doth betray Me.
Mt 26:47	And while he yet spake, lo, Judas, one of the twelve came and with him a great multitude with swords and staves from the chief priests and elders of the people.
Mt 26:50	Friend, wherefore art thou come?
Mt 26:52	Put up again thy sword into his place: for all they that take the sword shall perish with the sword.
Mt 26:53	Thinkest thou that I cannot now pray to My Father and He shall presently give Me more than twelve legions of angels?
Mt 26:54	But how then shall the scriptures be fulfilled, that thus it must be?
Mt 26:55	Are ye come out as against a thief with swords and staves for to take Me? I sat daily with you teaching in the temple and ye laid no hold on Me.

Mt 26:56	But all this was done, that the scriptures of the prophets might be fulfilled.
Mt 26:64	Thou hast said: nevertheless I say unto you, Hereafter shall ye see the Son of man sitting on the right hand of power and coming in the clouds of heaven.
Mt 26:69	Now Peter sat without in the palace: and a damsel came unto him saying, Thou also wast with Jesus of Galilee.
Mt 26:70	But he denied before them all, saying, I know not what thou sayest.
Mt 26:71	And when he was gone out into the porch, another maid saw him and said unto them that were there, This fellow was also with Jesus of Nazareth.
Mt 26:72	And again he denied with an oath, I do not know the man.
Mt 26:74	Then began he to curse and to swear, saying I know not the man. And immediately the cock crew.
Mt 26:75	And Peter remembered the word of Jesus, which said unto him, Before the cock crow, thou shalt deny Me thrice.

Mt 27:3   Then Judas, which had betrayed him, when he saw that he was condemned, repented himself and brought again the thirty pieces of silver to the chief priests and elders.

Mt 27:4   Saying, I have sinned in that I have betrayed the innocent blood. And they said, What is that to us? See thou to that.

Mt 27:6   And the chief priests took the silver pieces, and said, It is not lawful for to put them into the treasury, because it is the price of blood.

Mt 27:11   And Jesus stood before the governor: and the governor asked him saying, Art thou the King of the Jews? And Jesus said unto him, Thou sayest.

Mt 27:27   Then the soldiers of the governor took Jesus into the common hall and gathered unto him the whole band of soldiers.

Mt 27:29   And when they had platted a crown of thorns, they put it upon his head and a reed in his right hand: and they bowed the knee before him and mocked him saying, Hail, King of the Jews!

Mt 27:45   Now from the sixth hour there was darkness over all the land unto the ninth hour.

Mt 27:46   And about the ninth hour Jesus cried with a loud voice, saying, Eli, Eli, lama sabachtani?

That is to say, My God My God why hast Thou forsaken Me?

Mt 28:9	All hail.
Mt 28:10	Be not afraid: go tell My brethren that they go into Galilee, and there shall they see Me.
Mt 28:18	All power is given unto Me in heaven and in earth.
Mt 28:19	Go ye therefore and teach all nations baptizing them in the name of the Father, and of the Son and of the Holy Ghost:
Mt 28:20	Teaching them to observe all things whatsoever I have commanded you: and lo, I am with you alway, even unto the end of the world. Amen.
Rev 1:8	I am Alpha and Omega, the beginning and the ending, saith the Lord, Which is and Which was and Which is to come, the Almighty.
Rev 1:11	I am Alpha and Omega, the first and the last: what thou seest, write in a book and send it unto the seven churches which are in Asia: unto Ephesus and unto Smyrna and unto Pergamos and unto Thyatira and unto Sardis and unto Philadelphia and Unto Laodicea.
Rev 1:17	Fear not; I am the First and the Last:

Rev 1:18   I am He That liveth and was dead; and behold,
            I am alive for evermore, Amen: and have the
            keys of hell and of death.

Rev 1:19   Write the things which thou hast seen and the
            things which are and the things which shall be
            hereafter;

Rev 1:20   Thy mystery of the seven stars which thou
            sawest in My right hand and the seven golden
            candlesticks. The seven stars are the angels of
            the seven churches; and the seven candlesticks
            which thou sawest are the seven churches.

Rev 2:1   Unto the angel of the church of Ephesus write;
            These things saith He That holdeth the seven
            stars in His right hand, Who walketh in the
            midst of the seven golden candlesticks;

Rev 2:2   I know thy works and thy labour and thy
            patience and how thou canst not bear them
            which are evil and thou hast tried them which
            say they are apostles and are not and hast found
            them liars:

Rev 2:3   And hast borne and hast patience and for My
            name's sake hast laboured and hast not fainted.

Rev 2:4   Nevertheless I have somewhat against thee
            because thou hast left thy first love.

Rev 2:5   Remember therefore from whence thou art
           fallen and repent and do the first works; or else
           I will come unto thee quickly and will remove
           thy candlestick out of his place except thou
           repent.

Rev 2:6   But this thou hast, that thou hatest the deeds of
           the Nicolaitans, which I also hate.

Rev 2:7   He that hath an ear, let him hear what the Spirit
           saith unto the churches: To him that
           overcometh will I give to eat of the tree of life,
           which is in the midst of the Pardise of God.

Rev 2:8   And unto the angel of the church in Smyrna
           write. These things saith the First and the Last,
           Which was dead and is alive;

Rev 2:9   I know thy works and tribulation and poverty
           (but thou art rich) and I know the blasphemy of
           them which say they are Jews, and are not, but
           are the synagogue of Satan.

Rev 2:10   Fear none of those things which thou shalt
           suffer: behold, the devil shall cast some of you
           into prison, that ye may be tried; and ye shall
           have tribulation ten days: be thou faithful unto
           death, and I will give thee a crown of life.

Rev 2:11   He that hath an ear, let him hear what the Spirit
            saith unto the churches; He that overcometh
            shall not be hurt of the second death.

Rev 2:12   And to the angel of the church in Pergamos
            write; These things saith He Which hath the
            sharp sword with two edges;

Rev 2:13   I know thy works and where thou dwellest,
            even where Satan's seat is: and thou holdest
            fast My name and hast not denied My faith,
            even in those days wherein Antipas was My
            faithful martyr, who was slain among you,
            where Satan dwelleth.

Rev 2:14   But I have a few things against thee, because
            thou hast there them that hold the doctrine of
            Balaam, who taught Balac to cast a
            stumblingblock before the children of Israel to
            eat things sacrificed unto idols and to commit
            fornication.

Rev 2:15   So hast thou also them that hold the doctrine of
            the Nicolaitans, which thing I hate.

Rev 2:16   Repent; or else I will come unto thee quickly
            and will fight against them with the sword of
            My mouth.

Rev 2:17   He that hath an ear, let him hear what the Spirit
            saith unto the churches. To him that

overcometh will I give to eat of the hidden manna, and will give him a white stone and in the stone a new name written which no man knoweth saving he that receiveth it.

Rev 2:18 And unto the angel of the church in Thyatira write; These things saith the Son of God, Who hath His eyes like unto a flame of fire and His feet are like fine brass;

Rev 2:19 I know thy works and charity and service and faith and thy patience and thy works; and the last to be more than the first.

Rev 2:20 Notwithstanding, I have a few things against thee, because thou sufferest that woman Jezebel, which calleth herself a prophetess, to teach and to seduce My servants to commit fornication and to eat things sacrificed unto idols.

Rev 2:21 And I gave her space to repent of her fornication: and she repented not.

Rev 2:22 Behold, I will cast her into a bed and them that commit adultery with her into great tribulation, except they repent of their deeds.

Rev 2:23 And I will kill her children with death; and all the churches shall know that I am He Which

	searcheth the reins and hearts: and I will give unto every one of you according to your works.
Rev 2:24	But unto you I say, and unto the rest in Thyatira, as many as have not this doctrine and which have not known the depths of Satan, as they speak; I will put upon you none other burden.
Rev 2:25	But that which ye have already, hold fast till I come.
Rev 2:26	And he that overcometh and keepeth My works unto the end, to him will I give power over the nations:
Rev 2:27	And he shall rule them with a rod of iron; as the vessels of a potter shall they be broken to shivers: even as I received of My Father.
Rev 2:28	And I will give him the morning star.
Rev 2:29	He that hath an ear, let him hear what the Spirit saith unto the churches.
Rev 3:1	And unto the angel of the church in Sardis write; These things saith He That hath the seven Spirits of God and the Seven stars; I know thy works that thou hast a name that thou livest and art dead.

Rev 3:2   Be watchful and strengthen the things which
           remain, that are ready to die: for I have not
           found thy works perfect before God.

Rev 3:3   Remember therefore how thou hast received
           and heard and hold fast and repent. If therefore
           thou shalt not watch I will come on thee as a
           thief and thou shalt not know what hour I will
           come upon thee.

Rev 3:4   Thou hast a few names even in Sardis which
           have not defiled their garments: and they shall
           walk with Me in white: for they are worthy.

Rev 3:5   He that overcometh, the same shall be clothed
           in white raiment; and I will not blot out his
           name out of the books of life, but I will confess
           his name before My Father, and before His
           angels.

Rev 3:6   He that hath an ear, let him hear what the Spirit
           saith unto the churches.

Rev 3:7   And to the angel of the church in Philadelphia
           write: These things saith He That is Holy, He
           That is True, He That hath the key of David,
           He That openeth and no man shutteth and
           shutteth and no man openeth:

Rev 3:8   I know thy works: behold, I have set before
           thee an open door and no man can shut it: for

thou hast a little strength and hast kept My
word and hast not denied My name.

Rev 3:9   Behold, I will make them of the synagogue of
Satan, which say they are Jews and are not, but
do lie; behold, I will make them to come and
worship before thy feet and to know that I have
loved thee.

Rev 3:10   Because thou hast kept the word of My
patience, I also will keep thee from the hour of
temptation, which shall come upon all the
world, to try them that dwell upon the earth.

Rev 3:11   Behold I come quickly: hold that fast which
thou hast, that no man take thy crown.

Rev 3:12   Him that overcometh will I make a pillar in the
Temple of My God, and he shall go no more
out: and I will write upon him the name of My
God and the name of the city of My God,
Which is new Jerusalem, which cometh down
out of heaven from My God: and I will write
upon him My new name.

Rev 3:13   He that hath an ear, let him hear what the Spirit
saith unto the churches.

Rev 3:14   And unto the angel of the church of the
Laodiceans write: These things saith the

	Amen, the faithful and true Witness, the beginning of the creation of God;
Rev 3:15	I know thy works that thou art neither cold nor hot: I would thou wert cold or hot.
Rev 3:16	So then because thou art lukewarm and neither cold nor hot, I will spue thee out of My mouth.
Rev 3:17	Because thou sayest, I am rich and increased with goods and have need of nothing; and knowest not that thou art wretched and miserable and poor and blind and naked:
Rev 3:18	I counsel thee to buy of Me gold tried in the fire, that thou mayest be rich; and white raiment, that thou mayest be clothed, and that the shame of thy nakedness do not appear; and anoint thine eyes with eyesalve , that thou mayest see.
Rev 3:19	As many as I love, I rebuke and chasten: be zealous therefore and repent.
Rev 3:20	Behold I stand at the door and knock: If any man hear My voice, and open the door, I will come in to him and will sup with him and he with Me.
Rev 3:21	To him that overcometh will I grant to sit with Me in My throne even as I also overcame and am set down with My Father in His throne.

Rev 3:22   He that hath an ear, let him hear what the Spirit saith unto the churches.

Rev 16:15   Behold, I come as a thief. Blessed is he that watcheth and keepeth his garments, lest he walk naked and they see his shame.

Rev 21:6   It is done. I am Alpha and Omega, the Beginning and the End. I will give unto him that is athirst of the fountain of the water of life freely.

Rev 22:7   Behold, I come quickly: blessed is he that keepeth the sayings of the prophecy of this book.

Rev 22:12   And behold, I come quickly; and my reward is with Me, to give every man according as his work shall be.

Rev 22:13   I am Alpha and Omega, the Beginning and the End, The First and the Last.

Rev 22:16   I Jesus have sent Mine angel to testify unto you these things in the churches. I am the Root and the Offspring of David and the bright and morning Star.

Rev 22:20   Surely I come quickly. Amen. Even so come, Lord Jesus.

Rom 1:7   To all that be in Rome, beloved of God, called to be saints: Grace to you and peace from God our Father and the Lord Jesus Christ.

Rom 4:1   What shall we say then that Abraham our father, as pertaining to the flesh, hath found?

Rom 4:4   Now to him that worketh, is the reward not reckoned of grace, but of debt.

Rom 4:11   And he received the sign of circumcision, a seal of the righteousness of the faith which he had yet being uncircumcised: that he might be the father of all them that believe, though they be not circumcised; that righteousness might be imputed unto them also:

Rom 4:12   And the father of circumcision to them who are not, of the circumcision only, but who also walk in the steps of that faith of our father Abraham which he had being yet uncircumcised.

Rom 4:16   Therefore it is of faith, that it might be by grace; to the end the promise might be sure to all the seed; not to that only which is of the law, but to that also which is of the faith of Abraham, who is the father of us all.

Rom 4:17   (As it is written, I have made thee a father of many nations:) before Him Whom he believed, even God, Who quickeneth the dead and calleth those things which he not, as though they were.

Rom 4:18   Who against hope believed in hope that he might become the father of many nations, according to that which was spoken, So shall thy seed be.

Rom 6:4   Therefore we are buried with Him by baptism into death: that like as Christ was raised up from the dead by the glory of the Father, even so we also should walk in newness of life.

Rom 8:15   For ye have not received the spirit of bondage again to fear; but ye have received the Spirit of adoption, whereby we cry, Abba, Father.

Rom 9:10   And not only this; but when Rebecca also had conceived by one, even by our father Isaac:

Rom 15:6   That ye may with one mind and one mouth glorify God, even the Father of our Lord Jesus Christ.

Rom 15:30   Now I beseech you, brethren, for the Lord Jesus Christ's sake and for the love of the Spirit that ye strive together with me in your prayers to God for me;

Rom 15:31   That I may be delivered from them that do not believe in Judaea; and that my service which I have for Jerusalem may be accepted of the saints;

Rom 15:32   That I may come unto you with joy by the will of God, and may with you be refreshed.

Rom 15:33   Now the God of peace be with you all. Amen.

Think about the *truth* within the pages of this book. I learned more in two months of study with this chapel than I did going to church for ten years. Imagine!

To gain further understanding watch Shepherds Chapel daily for thirty days and make up your own mind and I believe you too will reach the same conclusion that I have, which is that this chapel teaches the word of God as God intended His word to be taught!

Call Shepherds Chapel
@ 1 800 643 4645

www.shepherdschapel.com

Call for this free tape (*a must have*) and viewing time in your area!

May God Bless you and your family now and always!

OTHER BOOKS BY THIS AUTHOR

Consider Truth
God's Truth

Consider Every Word
Of
Jesus Christ

Rapture Fact or Fiction
You Decide

Consider This
Before
Having a Child